Jack R. Taylor

After the Spirit Comes

Broadman Press/Nashville, Tennessee

Library of Congress Catalog Card Number: 73-93908
Dewey Decimal Classification: 248.4
Printed in the United States of America

To . . .
The Castle Hills Baptist Church of
San Antonio, Texas . . .

> . . . where it was my God-given privilege
> to serve as pastor for two hundred
> months . . . from 1957 to 1974 . . .
>
> . . . where I saw the manifestations of the
> coming of the Spirit in signs of real
> revival . . .
>
> . . . where in the midst of the adventures
> of a moving of God we began to see
> what
> happens . . . *After the Spirit Comes!*

Contents

Title Interpretation

God is omnipresent.
His Spirit is everywhere.
Technically he cannot go or come anywhere.
He is already there!

But there are times in the affairs of men when conditions are met in the spiritual realm and the Spirit of God moves in a fashion long remembered. There are times when the Holy Spirit, who has been there all along, manifests himself in people who come to blessing through brokenness. It is as if the Spirit *has just come.*

There are seasons in the lives of people who have been indwelt with the Spirit all along when the Spirit *resident* becomes the Spirit *reigning.* Jesus moves from a *peripheral* role in the life to a *prominent* role. It is as if the Spirit of God has only recently begun to move.

There are eras in the life of the church when there is a spiritual breakthrough and the blessed Spirit of God finds freedom in movement and manifestation. While he has been there all the time, it seems that he has just come.

In all of these instances the Holy Spirit is no more present and no more powerful than he was before. And in the event of a phenomenal spiritual awakening it isn't even that the Spirit is moving in a more decisive fashion. I am convinced that the Spirit is always on the move. The Bible never reveals him in a static position. But when folks decide to obey him and follow his leading, it seems indeed that he is moving more than ever!

So *After the Spirit Comes* is a description of that time which follows close to those times, seasons, and eras which mark the manifestations of the moving of the Holy Spirit.

God never leaves his children without direction and instruction. The Bible is filled with information from real-life experiences of the heroes of our faith—these are valuable to us in times like these. The prayer of the author is that this volume will relate the wealth of biblical material to situations and needs today in such a manner as to facilitate lasting victory *After the Spirit Comes.*

Introduction

These are days of consternation, chaos, and confusion. Not all of these conditions are outside the church. Much of what we see, as strange as it may seem, centers around what seems to have the marks of a genuine movement of God in our midst. That there have been stirrings in our world in the spiritual realm is without argument. Some of these are clearly of God and others as clearly of Satan. But some which bear the marks of both and could be either demand the gift of discernment for a final conclusion.

A casual observer of religious history, particularly that of revival movements, will note that these conditions are not altogether uncommon in times of the phenomenal movement of the Spirit. THERE HAS BEEN A MIGHTY MOVE OF GOD IN OUR WORLD IN CERTAIN AREAS. And in most of those areas there have been in attendance problems, excesses, and circumstances which are prone to bring the whole movement of God in that particular area into disrepute.

It is true that in the Great Awakening there was some emotional excess. In the great revival of the mid-nineteenth century there was some spiritual wreckage. Not all that occurred in the great Welsh Revival of the early years of the twentieth century was genuine. Doubtlessly some glorious events occurred in the revival in Indonesia, but well-meaning reporters and communication failures have placed the whole episode under a shadow. There is much *wild-fire* today *but there is fire.* No thinking person could wisely deny that there are manifold movings in the spiritual realms today. A few excesses and distortions do not neutralize the worth of an original work of God.

When the Holy Spirit of God seems to come in a new capacity, there is a crisis. When the Spirit moves, so does the enemy. When the devil cannot stop revival on the spot, he will attempt to prostitute it immediately, distort it gradually, or wreck it eventually. He is totally unscrupulous and is completely unbothered in using well-intentioned enthusiasts to do his bidding. Few of us have escaped those times when, unwittingly, we have, with twenty-four karat intentions, done the bidding of the enemy.

Many a person armed with a spiritual experience and limitless enthusiasm has walked in where angels fear to tread and has been used as a divisive and destructive force. Many others have come down from the mountain of emotional excitement, spent a few days of activity characterized more by enthusiasm than intelligence, and then found that inevitable letdown when doubt, discouragement, or depression attack. The unspoken feeling of many people back from a fresh spiritual encounter is, Now that my feelings have gone, where is God?

Many churches have been the scene of "the sound of a going" as of old when the army of David waited beneath the mulberry trees for signs that God had taken the field ahead of them. But after the initial stages pass problems arise. Pastors by the dozen are reeling dizzily before problems never before faced.

These pages are penned to pastors, churches, and all people who have begun to experience the *much more* in spiritual things only to find that the enemy has his version of the *much more* to seek to thwart the work of God.

This volume is a challenge to delve into the adventure of walking with God far past the beginning stages of excitement and enthusiasm. While these may accompany the relationship they are not always the leading actors in the drama.

This volume will seek to give *direction* to *dynamic*, positive *instructions* to *impact*, and *pertinence* to *power*. Any dynamic is potentially destructive and must have direction and design. I pray that these pages will throb with relevance to thousands who have thirsted and drunk at new fountains of spiritual vitality and desire to go on to a life-style led by the Spirit.

May the reader know by precept and experience the *dynamic*, the *delight*, and the *distress* which attend a period . . . AFTER THE SPIRIT COMES.

1
How it all Began

At Pentecost the Holy Spirit came as He had never come before. Jesus said "It is better for you that I go away, for if I go not away the Spirit will not come." The inference is that the presence of the Spirit is better than the bodily presence of Jesus.

The Holy Spirit is Christ without the limitations of the flesh and the material world. He is the Spirit of Truth, the Spirit of Witness, the Spirit of Power, the Spirit of Conviction, the Spirit of Revelation, the Spirit of Love, the Spirit of Glory, and the Spirit of Prophecy.

SAMUEL CHADWICK

"At that day ye shall know that I am in my Father, and ye in me, and I in you" (John 14:20).

"And when the day of Pentecost was fully come, they were all with one accord in one place. And suddenly there came a sound from heaven as of a rushing mighty wind, and it filled all the house where they were sitting. And there appeared unto them cloven tongues like as of fire, and it sat upon each of them. And they were all filled with the Holy Ghost, and began to speak with other tongues, as the Spirit gave them utterance" (Acts 2:1-4).

The Dawning of a New Day

The Holy Spirit has always been. He is not a new personality that appears on the day of Pentecost. We see the movement of the Holy Spirit first in Genesis 1:2, "and the Spirit of God moved upon the face of the waters." But now in this age the ministry of the Holy Spirit is such that we are justified in calling this age the *dispensation of the Spirit.* His movement has been recorded in every age from the beginning but now his capacities are unique, peculiar to this age, and of utmost significance.

Jesus had prepared his disciples for this day as thoroughly as such men could be prepared. We must not be impatient with them for their seeming shortsightedness. Had we known as little as they we would have been just the same. Jesus was physically with them. They depended greatly upon him. They did not welcome the fact that he one day might take his leave from them. They seemed to be deaf to such teaching that he would not always be with them. Surely he had come to establish his kingdom among them.

In John, chapters fourteen and sixteen, Jesus lets the disciples in on the plan for the future. He must leave. He would not, however, leave them without direction. He makes it clear that he would send them *One-Called-Alongside-Of*, another of like nature to himself. Jesus called him the Comforter (John 14:16; 15:26; 16:7—*Paraclete* . . . "the one called alongside"), "the Spirit of truth" (John 14:17; 15:26; 16:13), and "Holy Ghost" (John 14:26). He flatly said, *"But the Comforter, which is the Holy Ghost,* whom the Father will send in my name, he shall teach you all things, and bring all things to your remembrance, whatsoever I have said unto you."

It may be said then, without being irreverent, that the Holy Spirit is for us the presence of Jesus Christ, the spiritual presence of Jesus himself. A spirit or ghost is a disembodied presence. *The Holy Spirit is the presence of Jesus Christ himself.* Some have rightly referred to the Holy Spirit as the other *unlimited Jesus.*

This Is That

"But this is that which was spoken by the prophet Joel" (Acts 2:16). The next verse is a direct quote from Joel 2:28 which begins with the words: "And it shall come to pass in the *last days,* saith God, I will pour out of my Spirit upon all flesh."

The new Peter, now Spirit-indwelt and Spirit-filled, made such a statement as to leave no doubt about where they were in history and where we are. "THIS IS THAT . . .," he declared. We have been experiencing *THAT* for more than nineteen centuries. A new age had begun. We are in that age. What happened at Pentecost is vital to all of us today in the twentieth century. To deny it or disregard it is foolish. We should stand around that day in history until we begin to understand our heritage as God's children today.

Too many of us have lived too long on the wrong side of Pentecost. Pentecost has a way of validating Calvary, for it is the Holy Spirit who certifies the reality of the resurrected Christ and prepares the human heart as his abode.

When He Is Come

The official capacities of the Holy Spirit are made crystal clear in the discourses of Jesus to the disciples.

"He may abide with you forever" (John 14:16).

"He shall teach you all things" (John 14:26).

"He shall testify of me" (John 15:26).

"He will reprove the world of sin, and of righteousness, and of judgement" (John 16:8).

"He will guide you into all truth" (John 16:13).

"He will shew you things to come" (John 16:13).

"He shall glorify me" (John 16:14).

"He shall take the things of mine and shew them unto you" (John 16:14).

Jesus made another statement about the Spirit which is significant. He said, "For he dwelleth *with* you, and shall be *in* you." This is a vital distinction. Here are two words which imply togetherness but are different as to the nature of that togetherness. The Holy Spirit, at the moment when Jesus spoke these words, was *with* them because Jesus was *with* them. Jesus had already revealed his glorious secret when he said: "The words that I speak unto you, I speak not of myself; but the *Father that dwelleth in me*, he doeth the works" (John 14:10). Now Jesus promises the same arrangement with his followers that he had with the Father. The Spirit of God would dwell in them! In the same capacity that God indwelled him, he would indwell them! That was precisely the reason for the coming of the Spirit.

The term, *AT THAT DAY*, obviously refers to the day of Pentecost when the Spirit would come to begin this dispensation. On that occasion they would know by experience and by personal knowledge three vital things:

One, that Jesus Christ was in the Father.

Two, that they were in Jesus Christ.

Three, that Jesus Christ was in them (John 14:20).

This glorious promise materialized on the day of Pentecost when they were all filled with the Holy Ghost (Acts 2:4). They would be different who followed Christ. He was no longer *with* them in *bodily presence*. He was *in* them in *spiritual reality*. As he had promised, he had come to them in the Holy Spirit. "I will not leave you comfortless; *I will come unto you*" (John 14:18).

Such As I Have

A new brand of man walked along that day as Peter and John were on their way to the Temple to pray. Acts, chapter three, records the incident. A brief investigation of this first post-Pentecostal healing may serve to help us understand the glory of what happened when the Holy Spirit came to begin this dispensation.

Let us see first *the unanswerable paradox that detained them*. Peter and John were on their way to the Temple because it was the hour of prayer. They would not be alone. There would be others praying there because it was the hour of prayer according to their religion. Suddenly, within the sight of the gate of the Temple they found themselves detained. They were arrested by the sight of a *person* and the hearing of a *plea*. Here was a beggar pleading for alms. It was a clear paradox—a man whose life was so ugly in sight of a gate through which folks walked to worship God. Here was a man so ugly near a gate so beautiful. The paradox had not dawned upon the worshipers that made their way to the Temple daily. They could reach in tunic pocket and cast a coin in the lap of the wretched cripple without breaking stride or taking thought.

But here comes the new kind of man, the God-indwelt man. He cannot go by without inquiring into the situation. He cannot leave well enough alone. He looks and listens and eventually speaks.

Let us see second *the unexpected proclamation that described them*. In a statement Peter described the status of himself and John. They were broke. They were interested. They had something to give which was not money. I awakened one morning with four brief words pounding in my brain . . . SUCH AS I HAVE. They demanded investigation and then a proclamation. Peter said, "Silver and gold have I none; but SUCH AS I HAVE give I thee" (Acts 3:6). Those fastened themselves to my mind and would not let go. I began to see what Peter had was all that he needed. It was all that he had but it was enough. He did not have money, contacts, or influence. He did not have education, affluence, or ability. He did have *something* and it was *enough*. It was also all the cripple needed. He did not get what he *asked for* but he did get what he *needed*. May I ask and answer four brief questions?

Q. What was it that he had? A. He had the living power of the resurrected Christ residing in him ready to be released through him.

Q. Where did he get it? A. It was heaven's throne gift delivered to him at Pentecost as well as to all the others in the upper room when the Holy Spirit came. Jesus had come to live in him and them.

Q. Do we have it today? A. Emphatically, YES! All who have been born again are indwelt by the same Holy Spirit who came at Pentecost. The same baptism prophesied in every Gospel and repeated in Acts became ours at Pentecost. When we put our trust in Jesus Christ and turn from our sins, we are placed into him and he is placed into us.

Q. What should be happening in our lives today? A. If the same Holy Spirit lives in us who lived in the physical presence of Jesus, it is likely that he will be doing the same thing in us that he was doing in Jesus, that is, seeking the redemption of men. The Holy Spirit will render us redemptive. Jesus promised his followers that they would equal and exceed his works. "Verily, verily I say unto you, He that believeth on me, the works that I do shall he do also; and greater works than these shall he do; because I go unto my Father" (John 14:12).

Yes, they were men who were bereft of money, influence, and education, but their *such-as-I-have* was all that was needed.

Let us see third *the unexplainable power that distinguished them.* The power was unexplainable to man. The people were filled with wonder and amazement. Peter gave explanation by saying: "Ye men of Israel, why marvel ye at this? or why look ye so earnestly on us, as though by our own power or holiness we had made this man to walk. The God of Abraham, and of Isaac, and of Jacob, the God of our fathers, hath glorified his Son, Jesus . . . and his name through faith in his name hath made this man strong, whom ye see and know: yea the faith which is by him hath given him this perfect soundness in the presence of you all." (Acts 3:12-16) The power that distinguished them was the power of the name of Jesus. It was as if Jesus himself was standing there holding the cripple's hand. Indeed he was standing there in the person of Peter, and when Peter said, "In the name of Jesus Christ of Nazareth rise up and walk," all the power that was in that name, JESUS, came through.

Finally, and fourth we see the *undeniable proof that delighted them.* Peter and John walked into the Temple with a living sample of their ministry. Here was the man who had been laid at the gate of the Temple day after day and now here he was walking, and leaping, and praising God. This experience became a pulpit from which Peter gladly and immediately preached.

I have what Peter had. You have what he had if you are saved. You have the resurrected Christ living in your life. You and I may not have a lot of things but we do have this and this is all we need. We are indwelt of the Spirit of God who is the living Essence of Jesus in us. What of it? Read on!

After This, What?

What happens when these folks, patented at Pentecost, move out into the world? Trouble comes! Opposition arises! All sorts of unusual things begin to happen! Men would in times to come both reverence Pentecost and revile it. Some would shun it and others would build denominations over it. A few would foolishly try to duplicate it while others would if they could destroy it. And such it is with any moving of the Spirit of God.

There are two things which need to be remembered about Pentecost. One, what happened at Pentecost is not *repeatable* but it is *residual.* There is no way to repeat what happened at Pentecost nor is there a need to do so. Some seek to justify all modern-day tongue speaking in the languages of Pentecost by implying that it is the pattern for every experience of fulness. *If this were true then we would have to demand the sound of rushing wind and the cloven tongues of fire.* But what happened there is still with us. Because of it we can be born again and instantaneously indwelt with the Spirit of God. It is residual!

Two, what happened at Pentecost was not the *commencement* of a new *denomination* but the *coming* of a mighty *dynamic.* Jesus said, "Ye shall receive *power,* after that the Holy Ghost is come upon you: and ye shall be witnesses unto me both in Jerusalem,

14

and in all Judea, and in Samaria, and unto the uttermost part of the earth" (Acts 1:8).

That was the beginning of the day in which we live. This is how it all began. A casual acquaintance with what happened in the book of Acts following the initial coming of the Holy Spirit to this age of which we are a part will better equip us to understand and behave in times like these AFTER THE SPIRIT COMES.

2
Confessions
of
a
Pilgrim

This chapter seems to be a parenthesis and may well be. It seemed best to give a short report on a not-so-short pilgrimage far from finished but ever exciting.

JRT

It is said that honest confession is good for the soul. If that is true, I am about to do my soul a favor. I am absolutely sure of the fact that honest confession is good for other souls who are encouraged thereby to get honest about their own needs and hang-ups.

It is my policy, as it has been from the beginning, to be transparently honest even at the risk of being misunderstood. What you are about to read are perusings of a pilgrim with whom God is not finished yet. I love the little button which is worn on the lapels of many of the registrants at Bill Gothard's seminars. On the button are the letters P B P W M G I N F W M Y. The explanation of this abbreviation is "PLEASE BE PATIENT WITH ME, GOD IS NOT FINISHED WITH ME YET!" Hallelujah for that fact!

I do not have all the truth. I do not even understand all the truth I have. Some of it I am not ready to vocalize. I do have *some* of the truth. The truth that I do have has been lifting and liberating. I do have all of THE PERSON OF TRUTH which is Jesus Christ himself. He who is the Living Truth is always imparting himself to me through written truth in the Bible. With the Living Truth in my heart and Written Truth in my hand, I can through the eye-gate and ear-gate see and hear and thus come to a vital relationship with God through Jesus Christ by the Holy Spirit.

In my first book, *The Key to Triumphant Living,* I shared the joys of discovery and the adventures of living the blessed secret that Jesus Christ himself indeed indwells the life of every believer. In its sequel, *Much More,* I sought to share some of the principles by which the walk with him is enhanced and strengthened. In the third book, *Victory Over the Devil,* we took a side trip into the realm of spiritual warfare. In the fourth book, *One Home Under God,* I reported to you that the life of the Spirit really worked in the "nitty-gritty" of life's most intimate and trying relationships.

These books have been wonderfully received. You might as well know, however, that I have been *applauded* and *attacked, bragged on* and *bawled out, blessed* and *blamed,* and *thanked* and *spanked.* Of the making of books there is no end. This statement by the preacher in Ecclesiastes is certainly being proved true today. I, for one, intend to keep making contributions to keep the endless train going. I pray that the following reports will uncover to you comfort and blessing. Remember that they are not *expositions* of an *expert* but *perusings* of a *pilgrim.*

My Personal Prejudices

I was saved at the age of ten and almost immediately exposed to a type of religion that was quite frightening to me. The rantings and cavortings were at once both perturbing and puzzling. Added to this confusion was the known misconduct of the clergyman of this particular religion. This all made an indelible mark on my impressionable mind, a mark which was to stay for a long time. Most of the talk of this group centered around the Third Person of the Trinity, the Holy Spirit. Thus, almost without knowing it, there was built up inside of me a wall of prejudice regarding the Holy Spirit.

I knew that when I was converted the Holy Spirit came to indwell me, but I did not lose all my fears and hang-ups about him. When I thought of the Holy Spirit, my mind went back to those memorable visions of folks rolling, ranting, and raving all in the name of an experience with the Holy Spirit.

I do not ever remember hearing the term *being filled with the Holy Spirit* in a Baptist church during my years of growing up. I think if I had heard it I would have been frightened out of my wits lest I would catch what those folks had whose antics were so deeply etched on my memory.

I was faithful, however, with the passing years, to retain a desire to be all that God could make of a saved sinner. I do not ever remember being without a passion to be all that he wanted me to be. As time passed, I would read every book I could get my hands on that approached the subject of the Holy Spirit. I began to find that the older the book the more frequently was the subject of the Spirit discussed.

In my pilgrimage the point at which the hammer of God's reality struck the anvil of my recognition was the indwelling of the Person of Jesus Christ. At that time I was not Holy Spirit conscious, that is, I was more aware of the reality of Jesus than of the one (the Holy Spirit) who was making him real. Those were the days when the glory of the CHRIST-IN-ME revelation was so vital and vivid. What a restful and rewarding revelation . . . CHRIST WAS IN ME! His fellowship was precious. His word came alive in my heart. His presence was vivid and exciting. I did not know what was happening to me. I did know that life was taking a turn for the better.

About this time I was reintroduced to the concept of the fulness of the Holy Spirit. At the beginning I almost protested that it was Jesus, not the Holy Spirit, who lived in me. It was then that I noticed that slight but positive prejudice against the Holy Spirit still clinging to my heart. Wasn't it Jesus who was most important? And didn't the Bible say that the Holy Spirit would not speak of himself? At that point the Holy Spirit began to speak to my heart. Yes, Jesus was supremely important. Yes, the Holy Spirit would major on Jesus Christ and not on himself. But surely the one sent to make Jesus known was one who deserved my love and submission. In fact was he not himself the *presence* of Jesus sent to make the glorious *Person* of Jesus known? That night I fell in love for the first time with the Third Person of the Trinity! I can hardly explain it. There was joy unspeakable, a breakthrough in liberty, and a greater revelation of Jesus Christ. This was just the beginning!

The Pendulum Principle

Every active pendulum swings from one side to the other. It hangs for the slightest part of a second at one extreme only to swing to the farthest opposite and then to return again. This seems to be the principle under which we learn much of the truth that becomes a part of our lives.

We view and believe a vital part of truth and hang to it almost oblivious to any other truth and then swing to the opposite position to embrace truth that is not opposing but implementing. Then we discover that this is precisely how truth goes on, embracing all that is included from pole to pole of spiritual truth. In such a situation we have the pendulum of believing faith swinging in perfect symmetry over the whole spectrum of truth.

It must be remembered, however, that if the process is to continue, the pendulum cannot stop at either extreme or its purpose will be *distorted*. Neither can it stop in the middle or its purpose would be *dead*. Thus we need to know both sides of truth. We need to know of the atoning work of Christ as well as the sanctifying work of the Holy Spirit. We need to know of the love of God and of the justice of God. To refuse to swing is *death* to truth. To insist on swinging too far and staying is *distorting* to truth.

I, as others, have witnessed in my own life and teachings various swings to the extreme. I pray that I have been honest in my desire to be balanced in the application of truth.

The Tongues Trauma

The issue of speaking in tongues is not a new one to my mind. I witnessed what was supposed to be speaking in tongues when I was just a lad. I witnessed it but I never experienced it. For the greater part of the first twenty years of my relationship with Christ the practice of speaking in tongues was confined to small Pentecostal groups who were looked upon by most as fanatics. Then the practice began to jump denominational lines and has become in our day a major issue with thousands of reputable and respectable scholars standing at extremes to declare at once: "All tongues are of the devil!" and "Everybody must speak in tongues who is filled with the Spirit!"

I have been greatly bothered by this issue. I am as bothered by one extreme as I am the other. Without going into the various interpretations of Scripture, allow me to share with you the restful position to which God has led me. I have known what it is to be both intimidated and attracted by the modern movement which is characterized by the tongues trademark. I have moved all along the spectrum, saying at various times, "Lord, you wouldn't do this to me!" and "Lord, you wouldn't withhold this from me!" (Referring to tongues). I found myself increasingly "hassled," unconsciously giving the whole matter of tongues undue attention. I was as far from one group as I was from the other. I could not agree with those who said, "Nobody will!" and I could not agree with those who said, "Everybody must!" I have spoken with those who have advocated both sides with convincing zeal and not until I honestly restudied the Scripture and took my eyes off men did I come to a satisfying stance.

This is not the place for an exhaustive statement of what I believe the Bible teaches about tongues. I will make it brief by saying that NOBODY MUST, SOMEBODY MIGHT, I HAVEN'T! When on an occasion somebody *might* it will not call attention to itself, will not be divisive, and will not demand everybody to follow suit.

This stance will be unacceptable to both extremes. The truth is that I have been as open as I know how to be with both sides. At the same time I have been both avoided and accused by some in either camp. I have discovered, however, that if we can focus our eyes on Jesus and keep them there we can have respect for and fellowship with each other.

In the midst of this stance I do consider it wise to heed the warning of William G. Scroggie who said: "Thank God, we may and should be filled with the Spirit, with a fulness that means nothing less than a dethronement of self and an enthronement of Christ, or in the terminology of Paul, the reckoning of self to have died in Christ's death, and of ourselves newly alive in His resurrection. The craving today, on the part of many believers, for sensuous signs, is most unhealthy; it is destructive of sober Bible study, and invariably leads to pitiful extremes in belief and conduct. I feel compelled, therefore, to warn all seekers after fuller blessing against this unscriptural teaching about the Baptism of the Spirit and Tongues, lest such be led into darkness and doubt." [1]

I would, likewise, sound a warning against anyone so tightly fitting God into this or another dispensation that God would not be free to do and bestow what he sovereignly pleases.

The Demon Dilemma

In the midst of discovering spiritual truth and of the movings of God in an extraordinary manner, I became aware of the work of the devil. I never paid him much attention before. I knew who he was and I didn't like him but I never thought much about him. When the Spirit came in a time of reviving, the activity of the devil became rather decisive. Attacks became too frequent to be coincidental. We were not imagining things. The devil was alive! (I have never been convinced that he was *well* since what happened at Calvary! I believe him to be rather terminally ill! Strong but ill!) We began to study about the devil to prepare to stand against his wiles, as Paul exhorted. Our people began to discover that the believer really has authority over the devil in the name of Jesus. There are few truths as immediately rewarding as this one when applied.

I then asked God to teach me what he wanted me to know about demons. I really had no exciting desire to be aggressive in this area of study but if God had truth for me I wanted to know it. We began having strange encounters with people obviously oppressed with demonic powers. We had some rather dramatic confrontations and some equally dramatic liberations. More and more time began to be spent in counseling and working with the oppressed.

I wrote a book entitled *Victory Over the Devil*. It includes the basics regarding the devil, demons, angels, and Jesus Christ our Lord. While I believe that all that is in the book is true I believe that it is not all the truth. It is when we make a truth as if it were all the truth that we get into trouble.

Few people ever plunge into a study of the devil and demons without getting imbalanced at least temporarily. There is something about this area of truth that is particularly appealing to the human mind. I did not escape this pitfall.

The demon dilemma is as volatile and incendiary as the tongues trauma. We will be arguing the issue, "Can a Christian have a demon?" when Jesus comes. I find it wise for me not to enter into debate but to declare more vital issues. *The devil and his demons were defeated at Calvary.* Jesus Christ is Lord! Nothing that is under his feet is over my head! He that is in me is greater than he that is in the world!

While there are some cases of genuine demonic traffic, there are hundreds of others who are conveniently giving in to the flesh and *blaming it on demons.* In the former there can be deliverance from demons; in the latter, deliverance from the flesh. Our Lord has defeated the world, the flesh, and the devil.

Again, I find myself strangely standing in the middle . . . shot at, but still and satisfied. While some "go to seed" over finding demons under every chair and behind every frown, others with equally expensive error totally deny their existence and thus preclude the possibility of deliverance. I plead for balance.

The Healing Hassle

With the advent of Kathryn Kuhlman and other notables in the area of divine healing there comes another point of contention. Can everyone who is ill expect to be healed? Is healing in the atonement? These and other perplexing questions are being hurled about in our day and reactions reveal frayed nerves.

Again, it should be noted that when undue attention is given any area of truth imbalance results. If we are not careful, we will find ourselves more excited about removing demons or getting sickness healed than in bringing men to Christ.

I have had healings. In fact, I have been healed 100 percent of the time. (Unless I have an illness of which I am not aware!) Some of those healings have been dramatic and sudden. I was healed of asthma rather suddenly. The Lord healed a hurt toe almost immediately. But most of the times that I have been healed it has been according to the rules of recuperation which God placed within my body. They are no less miraculous than the sudden kind of healing. It is amazing to see a cut or a wound slowly and perfectly heal, the flesh making its own sutures and protective scar tissue.

God will heal most by the normal procedure of recuperation in time. He will heal a few in a dramatic fashion. Some will die sick and pass on into glory. Some will live with illness and rise over every pain and circumstance to become living examples of the fact that there is victory in Jesus!

I have prayed for people and they have been healed. I have witnessed the disappearance of growths that were awaiting surgery. I can confess to you the feeling of exhilaration that results from being used to pray for someone's healing and watching it happen. I could very easily succumb to the desire to make physical healing more important than it is. While I will still pray for the sick I affirm that the greatest endeavor among Christians is that of getting men with sin-sick souls to the Great Physician who heals for eternity.

Disciples and Divisions

I confess to you that this pilgrim is rather weary with all the talk about the things that make us different. It will suffice to give here an observation of the great Vance Havner. He related that if the three blind men Jesus healed gathered in the climate of today's religious divisiveness they would have problems. He featured the first blind man giving his testimony thusly: "Fellows, I will tell you, He touched me and I saw perfectly. It was wonderful! He touched me once and that was all!" Havner pictured the response of the second blind man: "Well, I'll tell you right now that you are not orthodox. He touched me and I saw, but not well. I saw men as trees walking. He touched me again and I saw every man clearly. If you are going to have a genuine experience you must have one like mine!" He then suggested that the third blind man might reply, "My observation is that neither of you had a genuine experience because you did not have an experience like mine. You see, he put spittle and clay together and rubbed it in my eyes. He then commanded me to go and wash in a pool. When I did what he said, I saw perfectly!" Vance Havner then amusingly suggested, "If those three blind men were here today we would have three denominations before the end of the week. We would have the ONE-TOUCH Church, the TWO-TOUCH Church, and the MUD-IN-THE-EYE Church!"

The significant thing about those blind men is that each of them in a marvelously unique manner passed from darkness into light. As long as the earth stands there will be differences in interpretations and terminology. We tend to find equal footing when we sing:

> Saved, by His power divine,
> Saved to new life sublime!
> Life now is sweet and my joy is complete,
> For I'm saved, saved, saved!

Back to Basics

I confess to you that I am rather simplistic. I have had my fling. I want to give equal time to all areas of truth that are vital but not undue time to one area. It's back to basics to me. The law was complicated. That was a part of the penalty of sin. The law is the schoolmaster which brought us to Christ . . . complex and demanding! But once we are brought to Christ it is simple.

What are the basics?

Christ died for sinners.

All men are sinners.

Christ died for all.

We are responsible to tell the story of His redeeming love.

Christ died *for* us on the cross, wants to live *in* us in vital life, and manifest himself *through* us in vital ministry.

He, living in us, is our hope of glory . . . becoming all that in the plan of God we were made to become.

Men can be born again of the Spirit, indwelt by the Spirit, and filled with the Spirit. The life-style of the Spirit will be characterized by Christlike conduct and character, loving and living, vitality and victory. The church's main business is to win men to Christ, teach them of Christ, and train them for Christ. These are the basics. Other areas of truth are vital as they attend the basics.

Wherever you and I go in our quest for truth I pray that our trend will always be BACK TO BASICS.

Thus, you have read some of the confessions of a pilgrim. A pilgrim is a traveler on a journey. Having looked back to where it all began let us go on to discover the delights that await us AFTER THE SPIRIT COMES.

3

The Pilgrim's Pitfalls

God has deliberately scattered along the pilgrim's path pitfalls and problems designed to shape, enlarge, and make prosperous. An opportunity to fail is an opportunity to succeed.

JRT

"Wherefore let him that thinketh he standeth take heed lest he fall" (1 Cor. 10:12).

There is a vast amount of spiritual fallout today and there promises to be more. With a new emphasis on the Holy Spirit and many people reporting a renewed relationship with God through the Spirit, there has also come a vast amount of spiritual wreckage. Some are satisfied to blame all of this on the emphasis of Holy Spirit truth and forsake it altogether. While there are some dangerous errors being promulgated in today's religious world it is equally dangerous to forsake areas of truth because of the abuses of others. Ian Thomas was right when he said that nothing so tended to spread error as unenlightened enthusiasm. On the other side it should be remembered that there is not a great deal of help from spiritless orthodoxy.

I have sought to deal in every volume I have written with the problems that relate to the pilgrim's life. This chapter will serve as a guide to later chapters, as well as a source or help in basic problems which face the traveler along the trail of truth.

The Problem of Problems

I am not supposed to have problems, I thought as I contemplated books written and sermons preached on victorious living. Problems are a sign of unspirituality, I suggested to myself. Nevertheless I had them! And the fact that I thought I was not supposed to have problems complicated the matter. I have discovered this to be a common dilemma among folks today who are going on with the Lord. They come to a turning point and the first days are glorious indeed. Emotions are high and blessings are manifold. Then there comes the letdown. It almost seems worse than before. Now they have two problems: one, the problem itself and, two, the fact that they are not supposed to have problems. (So they think!)

Well, one day I simply hauled off and told the Lord that I had problems. I did not receive from him a feeling of condemnation. I even told my friends and they did not think less of me. I began to relax and recognize that God never shields his people from problems but has a vital purpose in them. If we deny them, run from them, or rebel against them, we do not reap the benefits of our problems. I discovered another thing. When I admitted I had problems and laid aside my mask of certainty and confidence, other people came forth—comforted by my confessions—to comfort me.

If you have not discovered the exciting fact that problems are used by the Lord to bring heaven's blessings down to you, you are in for the time of your life. This subject is further dealt with in an ensuing chapter entitled "The Purpose of Problems." The chapter which follows it, "The Joseph Principle," will reinforce your faith in God's providence amid problems.

The Problem of Pride

"I've reckoned myself to be dead, but something is still alive and giving me trouble!" This is the common cry of the honest pilgrim. The first stages of the fresh coming of the Spirit were characterized by love, joy, Christ-consciousness, and a delightful unconsciousness of self. It is almost as if self is gone forever. But alas, there it is . . . not dead, not even wounded, but very much alive! Disappointment and disillusionment abound. Self has ascended the throne. Pride has come calling. The worst thing about it is that we did not think it was any longer there. It is ever so subtle.

We can be pride-filled over the strangest things . . . a time of freedom in speaking, of power in prayer, and effectiveness in counsel. Pride can develop over usefulness in spiritual matters.

Your self is not dead. You may have reckoned it so mistakenly, but it is still alive. Paul said in Romans 6:11: "Reckon ye also yourselves to be dead indeed *unto sin,* but *alive unto God* through Jesus Christ our Lord." There is a termination to the relationship of sin's domination but self is still alive and should be reckoned thus in the commencement of a new relationship *unto God through Christ.*

"Now That I'm Spiritual" is the title of a later chapter which is pointed toward honest folks who, in their own eyes, have all of a sudden become intensely "spiritual" and have problems finding fellowship with folks as "spiritual" as they.

The Problem of Presumption

The Bible is filled with people who committed the sin of presumption. *Abraham* presumed when he lied about Sarah being his sister. *Moses* presumed too much when he struck the rock with the rod instead of speaking to it as he was commanded. *Samson* was presumptuous when he expected to come and go as before only to find that his power was shorn with his hair.

There is a terrible tendency among Christians today to so categorize God that we know exactly when and how he is going to come through. We have him neatly fitted into patterns and have developed an expertise in predicting his behavior. Then tragedy strikes . . . tragedy which makes no sense. How do you explain this? We are awestruck and sober. We learn again that his ways are not our ways and his thoughts are not our thoughts. We are ready to exclaim with Paul: "O the depth of the riches both of the wisdom and knowledge of God! How unsearchable are his judgements, AND HIS WAYS PAST FINDING OUT" (Rom. 11:33).

"When God Doesn't Come Through" is a chapter which will help those who have put God on a schedule and found out that he paid little attention. There are times when God doesn't come through. We should be ready for those times.

The Problem of Discouragement

One of the devil's favorite and most used tools is that of discouragement. It can paralyze the strongest and cripple the mightiest. But isn't discouragement supposed to be done with after the Spirit takes over? God is obliged to bring us to live right next to our weakness that we might know his strength. He parks us next to our failures so that we might experience his success. The gospel is good news but it is *unheeded* good news until we believe the bad news. The bad news is that I am a sinner; the good news is that Christ is the sinner's Savior. The bad news is that I cannot live the Christian life; the good news is that he can! If I never believe the bad news, the good news is not good news.

There is a possibility that temporary discouragement may be extremely beneficial. On the other hand some discouragement is the result of the dashing of fleshly hopes, of expecting too much of the world.

Never was a man any more discouraged than Elijah in a period immediately following a great move of the Spirit. Fire had come to the mountaintop in response to his prayer and yet a few days later we find him in the pit of gloom. An ensuing chapter entitled "Under the Juniper Tree" will minister to those who often become discouraged.

The Problem of Compromise

The manifestations of the movings of God come at the price of man's genuine repentance. In times of spiritual reviving God entrusts abundant blessing. Solomon's wealth was a symbol of God's blessings and approval. When folks saw the splendour of his kingdom, they glorified the Lord.

But one day the glory of that kingdom faded. The king who followed Solomon might have returned it to its former glory but instead he compromised.

How easy it is when the glory is gone to use the same words as if the glory of former days is still present. We may sing the same songs, recite the same Scripture passages, and repeat the same rituals, but all are alike incapable of power and pertinence.

What we do when we witness the glory fading is of utmost importance. The chapter "Shields of Brass for Shields of Gold" will be of profit to all who ever considered compromise or who ever succumbed to it.

The Problem of Consistency

"O consistency, thou art a virtue!" I seem to start well and move along for a while—then inconsistency sets in. Regardless of the nature of the beginning, all is lost unless consistency can be achieved. We soon discover in the spiritual realm that the human frame is characterized by *consistent inconsistency.*

After the Spirit comes, the human leanings do not leave. How do we develop our lives along the lines of the Spirit? While the fulness of the Spirit is an experience, there is also a growth factor. The experience of being filled with the Spirit is the *commencement;* the growth relationship brings *consistency.*

For those of us who have consistency problems (and who doesn't?) I have entered a chapter entitled "The Rod of God." Another chapter that will speak to this problem is "Walking on the Water."

The Problem of Pressures

Pressures do not relax with the coming of the Spirit. In fact they seem to accelerate. Often with a new move of God there come problems. I have a friend who preached a sermon under the title "Receive Ye the Holy Spirit and Trouble!" That is more often than not the case. Are there pressure points in your life? Have you mistakenly thought that consecration would alleviate all the pressure of life? Have you lately noticed in the Scriptures that God's people were under constant pressure? Many of the psalms were written under pressures that are obvious to the reader. The prophets ministered in times of distress. Much of the ministry of Jesus and his disciples was carried on under threats. All of Paul's epistles were written under duress. A chapter to follow, "Faith for the Fiery Furnace," will help you see how God uses pressures to reveal his glory in his Son.

The Problem of Direction

"Whither from hither?" is a vital question. Everybody who has begun with Christ wants to go on but deciding where "on" is often becomes a problem in itself.

Many folks who are experiencing spiritual deepening find themselves going in the direction of isolation. Those in *isolation* cannot be ministers of *consolation*. There is such an emphasis today on spiritual deepening that some seem to be getting so deep they are sunk! They are sunk to evangelistic zeal. They are sunk to understanding helpfulness. They are sunk to everything but their own spiritual "depth."

Dynamic without *direction* is *destructive.* This is the reason that in times immediately following great movings of the Spirit there seem to frequently occur emotional and spiritual breakdowns. Proper emphasis on direction of ministries would solve much of the problem of such unwelcome fallout.

Three chapters will serve to give a sense of direction. These three chapters give the three vital directions in spiritual life. *The* church's greatest *ministry* speaks of the *upward* ministry of prayer. "Spiritual Footwashing" speaks of the ministry inward while "Let's Prioritize And Evangelize" speaks of the outreach of the church.

So much for the pitfalls and problems of the pilgrim. Praise the Lord for them all. The truth that gathers around each of them will prepare us for the journey onward!

4
The Purpose of Problems

God does not keep a man immune from trouble; He says, "I will be with him in trouble." It does not matter what actual troubles in the most extreme form get hold of a man's life. Not one of them can separate him from his relationship with God. We are "more than conquerors in all these things."

OSWALD CHAMBERS

"O our God, wilt thou not judge them? for we have no might against this great company that cometh against us; neither know we what to do; but our eyes are upon thee" (2 Chron. 20:12).

"These things I have spoken unto you, that in me ye might have peace. IN THE WORLD YE SHALL HAVE TRIBULATION: but be of good cheer; I have overcome the world" (John 16:33).

One of the clearest promises of Jesus to us is that we shall have problems. The Bible is a book filled with people with problems. The Christian and his problems comprise one of the most critical areas in the world. Here the devil wreaks more havoc than anywhere. Most Christians basically misunderstand their problems. Many are somehow led to believe that a sellout to Christ will lead to a problem-free existence.

When the Christian begins to believe the truth about his problems the glory of God comes into view. The truth about our problems is that they are the source of our prosperity, the means of our spiritual advancement.

Do you remember the two basic attitudes of the children of Israel toward their problems, namely the giants in the land? The majority quaked in their boots when the report came back that there were cities walled to the sky and giants in whose sight they were as grasshoppers. Listen to the response of the faithless: "And all the congregation lifted up their voice, and cried; and the people wept that night. And all the children of Israel murmured against Moses and against Aaron: and the whole congregation said unto them, Would God that we had died in the land of Egypt! or would God we had died in the wilderness! Let us make a captain, and let us return unto Egypt" (Num. 14:1-2,4).

They completely panicked before their problems. There was no evidence in their reaction that the Lord was their God!

Then Joshua and Caleb spoke: "The land which we passed through to search it, is an exceeding good land. If the Lord delight in us, then he will bring us into this land, and give it us; a land which floweth with milk and honey. Only rebel not ye against the Lord, neither fear ye the people of the land; for they are bread for us: their defence is departed from them, and the Lord is with us: fear them not" (Num. 14:7-9). Did you get it? THEY ARE BREAD FOR US! One group looked at their problems and saw *panic*. Caleb and Joshua looked at the same problems and saw *purpose*. What do you see in your problems?

Now, let us come to the case at point. Jehoshaphat was the son of Asa but he walked not in the ways of wickedness of his father. The Word says that he walked in the first ways of his father David (2 Chron. 17:3). Under the leadership of Jehoshaphat there was real revival. "[He] sought to the Lord God of his Father [David], and walked in his commandments, and not after the doings of Israel. Therefore the Lord stablished the kingdom in his hand; and all Judah brought to Jehoshaphat presents; and he had riches and honour in abundance" (2 Chron. 17:4-5).

It was a time of unprecedented blessings both spiritually and materially. The king cleaned out the places of heathen worship. He arranged that the Law of God should be taught throughout the land. The kingdom grew so great that nations around him were afraid to war against him. Though he mistakenly joined forces with wicked King Ahab and disregarded the advice of the prophet of God, he came back to Jerusalem in peace. He had learned a lesson. And now would come the big test!

First, notice *the conditions when the crisis came.* He had sought the Lord, exalted his Word, and led his people in obedience to the Word. A genuine time of renewal had come for the nation. The Spirit of God visited the king. "And the Lord was with Jehoshaphat" (2 Chron. 17:3). A great army was built up and Jehoshaphat was exceedingly great (2 Chronicles 17:12, 13).

Second, see *the crisis.* You wouldn't call this a minor crisis! The Moabites and the Ammonites and others were invading the land and were bent on destroying Jehoshaphat (2 Chron. 20:1-2). It was a *severe* crisis in that it involved the very existence of the nation and the life of the king. It was an *urgent* crisis in that the armies were already in Engedi at that moment.

Third, see *the center of the issue.* First Jehoshaphat did the human thing. He feared. This is an entirely normal reaction. It is generally the first reaction in a crisis. It is the second reaction that usually tells the story. What you do after that first moment is the turning point. *He set himself to seek the Lord!* A man is more prone to do this when he is in practice. This was not the first time that the king had sought the Lord. It had become a habit of his life. The more you make a habit of seeking the Lord, the more likely you will be to seek the Lord when problems come. He sought the Lord and he immediately began to reckon on the God of heaven instead of the problems. He rehearsed and vocalized his faith. Listen to his profession of faith:

"Are you not God in heaven?"

"Do you not rule over the kingdoms of the heathen?"

"Is not power and might in your hand so that none can stand against you?"

"Are you not our God who drove out the inhabitants of the land before thy people Israel and gave it to the seed of Abraham thy friend forever?"

"If, when evil comes upon us, as the sword, judgement, or pestilence, or famine, we stand before this house, and in thy presence, (for thy name is in this house) and cry unto thee in our affliction, *then thou wilt hear and help.* (See 2 Chron. 20:6-7,9.)

Fourth, witness *the concentration of his faith.* Listen to the final word of Jehoshaphat to the Lord: "O our God, wilt thou not judge them? For we have no might against this great company that cometh against us; neither know we what to do; BUT OUR EYES ARE UPON THEE" (2 Chron. 20:12). This is precisely where a problem begins to turn into prosperity. And this is precisely where most of us lose out in our problems. It is a matter of transferring the problem from our hands into his. Many of us engage in problem-centered praying. That is, we reckon more with the problem than anything else. Jehoshaphat engaged in God-centered praying. He turned his eyes away from the problem and unto the Lord. OUR EYES ARE UPON YOU! He talked with God, left the issue with God, and heard from the Lord.

God's word to him was: "Be not afraid nor dismayed by reason of this great multitude; for the battle is not yours, but God's" (2 Chron. 20:15). Let that final word vibrate down through the corridors of your soul . . . NOT YOURS BUT GOD'S! NOT MINE BUT HIS! If we could but be convinced that the battle is the Lord's, the victory would soon ensue.

Fifth, hear *the commands from the Lord*. The first command was, "Be not afraid nor dismayed." Fear and dismay encourage the enemy and hinder the Lord. Here they were apparently facing the battle of their lives. After Jehoshaphat heard from God, he said, "Believe in the Lord your God, so shall ye be established; believe his prophets, so shall ye prosper" (2 Chron. 20:20).

Our task is simple in the crises which confront us. Our problems are not threats but opportunities to see the God of heaven in action. He not only allows us to have problems but through the problems he desires to make us rich.

Sixth, see *the conflict in which they were engaged*. Of all things, they went into battle praising. The Lord had told them that they would not have to fight. All that was left to do was to praise. Their song was, "Praise the Lord; for his mercy endureth forever" (2 Chron. 20:21). The result was that God set "ambushments" against the enemy and they destroyed themselves.

Seventh, see *the children of God cashing in*. When the battle was over and all the enemy to the last man was slaughtered, the valley was strewn with wealth. Problems had been transformed unto prosperity. That is what praise will do! The valley that might have run deep with the blood of God's children became known as Berachah, the valley of blessing.

God has blessings for you beyond your imagination. The only manner in which he can convey those blessings to you is to create a need, a problem, a circumstance which demands dependence. The existence of the need presupposes the supply. God, being who he is, could never allow a need beyond his capacity to supply. The greater the need the greater the blessing.

What kind of situation do you find yourself facing right now? Have you rebelled against it, or have you turned your eyes away from the problem to him who ordered it for you for a blessing?

After the Spirit comes, God can begin to trust you with problems you could not stand before. They are not indications of the displeasure of God with your life but proof of his love in entrusting such blessings to you. The purpose of problems is the glory of God. Obey the Lord in the midst of your distresses and God will work a miracle of blessing in you.

5

The Joseph Principle

Careless seems the great Avenger; history's pages but record
One death-grapple in the darkness twixt old systems and the Word;
Truth forever on the scaffold, Wrong forever on the throne,—
Yet that scaffold sways the future, and, behind the dim unknown,
Standeth God within the shadow, keeping watch above his own.

JAMES RUSSELL LOWELL

"And they . . . sold Joseph to the Ishmeelites for twenty pieces of silver: and they brought Joseph into Egypt" (Gen. 37:28).

"For God did send me before you to preserve life" (Gen. 45:5).

"And God sent me before you to preserve you a posterity in the earth, and to save your lives by a great deliverance" (Gen. 45:7).

Anytime there is a move of God there is a counter move of Satan. Anytime there rises a man of God there rises against him opposition. God does not preclude it but rather makes it redemptive and enhancing. There is no story in the Bible which more perfectly proves this fact than the story of Joseph. God saw to it that every needed detail was in the story of Joseph. The report is full, covering ten chapters in Genesis.

Joseph's biography is given in Hebrews 11:22: "By faith Joseph, when he died, made mention of the departing of the children of Israel; and gave commandment concerning his bones."

I want to introduce to you the *Joseph principle*. It is a principle that affirms utter confidence in the ability of God to see his purpose through, despite anything that happens. God often takes the tools

36

fashioned by the devil with destruction in mind and makes of them wonderful sources of blessing for his children. In spite of and, in fact, because of what the devil did in the story of Joseph the final result is redemption!

The *Joseph principle* takes four great facts into account:

One, the overwhelming wickedness of Man.

Two, the overseeing providence of God.

Three, the overcoming obedience of Joseph.

Four, the overruling plan of God.

The Overwhelming Wickedness of Man

The principle which faces us takes reality into account. Spiritual reality demands that we recognize the wickedness of man. If we recognize it, we will have difficulty trusting man. This will leave all our trust for the Lord and him alone. Although Jesus was betrayed by men, he was never suspicious, never bitter. He despaired of no one. If we trust wholly in the Lord, neither will we despair of anyone. The adversary was so bent on destroying Joseph that he followed him into Egypt where the conspiracy continued.

See the overwhelming wickedness of man, first in *the depravity of Joseph's brothers.* They hated him because his father loved him. They could not speak a peaceful word to him. Isn't that just like unredeemed human nature? He dreamed a dream, obviously from the Lord, and shared it with his brothers. This aroused even more envy and hate. When he visited them in the fields, they plotted violence against him and eventually sold him as a slave into Egypt. Their wickedness is further revealed in their plot to deceive the father and declare Joseph dead.

More of man's innate wickedness is revealed in *the deceit of Potiphar's wife.* The adversary is not through with his attempts to destroy the man of God. The wife of Joseph's master made advances toward him. Day after day he refused her, vowing unswerving loyalty to his master. Finally, on an occasion she found him alone and caught him by the garment. As he fled he left his garment in her hand. She then proceeded to lie about Joseph which resulted in his being put into prison a condemned man.

Then we have *the disrespect of the liberated butler.* You will remember that while in prison Joseph was elevated to the position of keeper of the prison. In due time the king's butler and baker were placed in the prison under the authority of Joseph. Each of them had a dream. Joseph interpreted the dreams, and as he had interpreted so it happened. The baker was executed and the butler was liberated. To the butler Joseph said, "But think on me when it shall be well with thee, and show kindness, I pray thee, unto me, and make mention of me to Pharoah, and bring me out of this house" (Gen. 40:14). But as quickly as the butler was liberated he forgot. "Yet did not the chief butler remember Joseph, but forgot him" (Gen. 40:23).

The Overseeing Providence of God

All the while, unknown to anyone, God was keeping close watch over his investments and guarding his interests.

The providence of God was overseeing the whole affair. This meant several things. First, it meant that God's *presence* was involved. "And the Lord was with Joseph and he was a prosperous man" (Gen. 39:2). It was obvious to Joseph's master that God was with him. "And his master saw that the Lord was with him, and that the Lord made all he did to prosper in his hand" (Gen. 39:3). Second, it meant that God's *persistence* was involved. Joseph was cast into prison because of the deceit of his master's wife, but God persisted. "But the Lord was with Joseph, and showed him mercy, and gave him favour in the sight of the keeper of the prison" (Gen. 39:21). The butler forgot but God did not! Third, the *peace* of God was involved. There is about the whole story an atmosphere of peace. God would see him through. He could thus rest in peace. And that he did.

The Overcoming Obedience of Joseph

God's providence needs his children's obedient cooperation. Joseph was obedient to God in every circumstance. He was not bitter over being sold into slavery. There is never registered a note of hatefulness in any of the circumstances which surrounded him. He was faithful to his master, Potiphar, in spite of the repeated advancements of Potiphar's wife. He was faithful to use his God-given ability to interpret the dreams of the baker and the butler. He continues faithful and obedient until at last he was liberated from *prison* and lifted to *prominence* . . . the prime minister of Egypt!

Obedience is the basic ingredient in *overcoming*. All the foes of God cannot unseat the man who observes obedience as his first and last qualification for usefulness.

The Overruling Plan of God

The plan of God came through all the conspiracies of the adversary. God's plan is reflected first in Joseph's *prominence*. It was unsought and unbought as far as Joseph was concerned but carefully prearranged by the God of heaven. God's plan is seen next in Joseph's *purpose*. He had no doubt about that purpose by the time his brothers came. Pharoah had a dream and could find no one to interpret. The butler at last remembered, and Joseph was called from prison to interpret the dream. When the truth was known about the seven good years and the seven years of drought, Joseph was made prime minister of Egypt. God will go to any measure to elevate anyone whose elevation will bring glory to His name.

God's plan is again seen in Joseph's *proclamation*. In the moving scene in Genesis 45, Joseph sends everyone out of the room except his brothers and breaks into tears. He then confesses his true identity to his brothers. His proclamation is, "God did send me before you to preserve life" (Gen. 45:5). He was saying, "You didn't do it—God did! It wasn't evil—it was good!"

Finally, God's plan is reflected in Joseph's *proof*. When the brothers reported to their father that Joseph was alive, he could not believe. He had mourned the death of Joseph for twenty-two years. Joseph had disappeared when he was seventeen. He was thirty when he stood before Pharaoh to become the prime minister of Egypt. Seven years of plenty had passed and two years of the famine had come and gone. That made Joseph thirty-nine years old. Can you imagine the emotion-charged atmosphere when Jacob's heart fainted within him at the possibility of seeing his beloved son. The proof of Joseph's being alive came when Jacob saw the wagons sent by Joseph. The spirit of Jacob revived, and he said: "It is enough; Joseph my son is yet alive; I will go and see him before I die" (Gen. 45:28).

What an ending to a pathos-filled story! God is working out his plan for this muddled-up world. It may seem to be staggering but it is plodding on toward the purpose of God. The *Joseph principle* declares that God may not always be obvious in his presence and providence but he will win out in the end! Indeed Paul was right when he said: "And we know that all things work together for good to them that love God, to them who are the called according to his purpose" (Rom. 8:28). Deposit the *Joseph principle* in your heart. You will need it sooner than you expect!

6
Now
That
I'm
Spiritual

Spirituality, like humility, flees before self-consciousness. The enemy knows that the best way to wreck spirituality is to bring it to notice. Supposed or presumed spirituality is false spirituality. The more spiritual one becomes the less conscious he is of himself and the more conscious of THE HOLY ONE!

JRT

"Peter answered and said unto him, Though all men be offended because of thee, yet will I never be offended" (Matt. 26:33).

"Peter saith unto him, Lord, dost thou wash my feet? Thou shalt never wash my feet" (John 13:6,8).

When there is a great move of God, there is generally a breaking of emotional patterns. There is a great joy and there is great excitement. There are deep feelings and definite resolutions.

Peter, upon hearing Jesus say that they all would be offended because of him (speaking of his coming death), reflected a premature confidence in his own spirituality. Everybody else might be offended but not Peter. He seems to feel that he is made out of a different kind of stuff than all the rest. It is this kind of subtle pride that is the downfall of many a person. Everyone who has had the experience of coming to the end of themselves and the joy of a surge of new life has vowed that they could never backslide again.

That "now-that-I'm-spiritual" feeling has at one time or another come upon us all. We have all of a sudden become intensely spiritual. Everyone else around us seems commonly carnal in comparison. It is then that God is obliged to show us himself and thus ourselves. Many a person has mistaken an experience in which he thought he met God for one in which he merely met a new estimation of himself. You can always tell the difference. The man who has met God has said, "Woe is me!" The man who has merely met a new idea of his own spirituality is ready to bear testimony of himself.

In this mini-chapter I want to simply put down for your consideration the marks of false spirituality and the marks of true spirituality.

False Spirituality

First of all, false spirituality is built almost entirely on feelings, moods, impressions, and imaginations. These are all sense-oriented. The five senses reign supreme. In times of worship or prayer the vitality of the experience is measured by what happens that registers along the line of the senses. What do I hear, feel, taste, see, or smell? Beware when you are disappointed in the lack of manifestations by which your feelings are reassured in worshiping God. False spirituality begins to develop when we become more conscious of our feelings than we are of the glory of God as revealed through his Word.

Second, false spirituality is experience-centered. For its perpetuation, it is dependent on continued experiences or encounters. In these experiences visions sometimes occur, sensations and impressions are frequent, and the voice of God is said to be heard in specific and personal detail. "God told me thus and so!" is not an uncommon word heard among folks today. God has spoken in his Word. The canon of Scripture has long since been closed. God does not rely on the senses of man, or he could give revelations to a natural or unredeemed man. "The natural man receiveth not the things of the Spirit of God" (1 Cor. 2:14). Any message that God has to convey to us he is going to convey in such a way that faith is required to receive it.

Though being filled with the Spirit is an experience, it is a great deal more. There will be times when God will be obliged to shut us up to himself with no feelings, no emotions, and no experiences to reassure us . . . only faith in his unchanging nature.

Third, false spirituality is self-conscious. There are new developments in the areas of interpersonal relationships which call for undue attention on one's self. There is an emphasis on discovering one's true personhood. Acceptance in the group is substituted for acceptance with God. Self-acceptance is majored upon. In other areas spiritual gauges are set up to certify one's spirituality. The report of gifts, times of great usefulness, visions, or revelations are important in measuring where one is in his spirituality. Feelings of elation and happiness are very important. Feelings of spirituality (whatever that is) cause delusions of grandeur.

Fourth, false spirituality is condescending. "Now that I'm spiritual where can I find someone who is as spiritual as I am with which to fellowship. My church is not spiritual enough for me. My minister cannot help me because I am more spiritual than he. God bless all those poor, unspiritual people." Pride is such a subtle thing because it wears so many masks and can develop in any circumstance. It is most subtle and dangerous when it arises in the spiritual realm.

Fifth, false spirituality is usually undisciplined. Being accustomed to depend on feelings, moods, and impressions there is not much dependence on regularity of discipline.

Sixth, false spirituality has a tendency to be impatient. Intolerance of another point of view or another person's position is often reflected. A lack of love and gentleness toward those "less spiritual" is often seen.

Seventh, false spirituality is easily disillusioned. By right of the fact that it depends upon visions and voices, sensations and impressions, there is a natural problem waiting. An impression is received that something is going to happen. It does not occur and disillusionment results. Dramatic disappointments, brought on by expectations that God did not give, often serve to all but wreck the faith of the well-intentioned.

Now it must not be concluded that false spirituality is so clearly defined that it can be easily detected and immediately eradicated. The conditions that I have named have at one time or another been tendencies of us all. As I have put them down, my own heart has asked, Can anyone be genuinely spiritual? The answer to that question is an emphatic, NO! *We can't but he can!* It is the reckoning of the self-life dead unto sin and alive unto God through Christ that renders us capable of allowing him to behave as he desires in us.

True Spirituality

Obviously true spirituality is characterized by the opposites of false spirituality.

True spirituality is not reliant on feelings and emotions for its continuation. It may have as many feelings of elation and joy but they are not the final test.

True spirituality is truth-centered and not experience-centered. The truth of the Word of God is enough. It does not wait on the approval of our senses for certification. True spirituality is Christ-conscious and not self-conscious. Oswald Chambers said, "The initiative of the saint is not towards self-realization but towards knowing Christ. The Holy Spirit is determined that we shall realize Jesus Christ in every domain of life, and He will bring us back again and again to the same point until we do. Self-realization leads to the enthronement of work; whereas the saint enthrones Jesus Christ in his work." "That I may know him . . ." is the continuous passion of true spirituality.

True spirituality is never condescending for in it there is the recognition of the unholiness of man and the holiness of God. If I can remember that it is by his mercy that I am not consumed, I will never look down on others.

True spirituality manifests itself in kindness and patience toward others. It is unoffended and unoffendable love. It has nothing to prove and thus is not embittered when refused. It has nothing to lose and thus is not disheartened by threats. It cannot be disillusioned because it is centered on Jesus Christ and he is the same, yesterday, today, and forever. It is disciplined because it depends on the Written Word and the Living Word for sustenance and must stay in close touch with both.

What is true spirituality? It is simply Jesus Christ minding his own business inside my spirit, soul, and body. It is Jesus Christ acting like himself. It is the Holy Spirit producing the natural fruit of the Spirit. It is the self-life continually dying that the Christ-life might be continually living.

There is no true spirituality apart from Jesus Christ. He is all and in him I am complete. (See Col. 3:11; 2:10.)

7

When God Doesn't Come Through

On the way back from the revival you might get ready for those times when God chooses not to say anything in your hearing or do anything in your seeing. You may learn later that more was accomplished during those times than all others put together.

JRT

There are times when God doesn't come through! You will ever be creating situations to make God look good in the evaluations of men if you declare that he always comes through. God many times cuts across our expectations and schedules, and we are shocked. There are other times when we declare that he will surely answer. Doesn't he know that this is the date of the deadline? Is he not aware that I must have an answer today? Didn't I get peace in prayer that the matter would be settled this very day?

If you intend to go on with God, prepare for those times when he chooses to wean you from his having to always come through at your appointed time. If he can trust you to trust him, he will put you in tight places where your soul is enlarged and your vision is widened. Then you will be able to delight more in *who he is* than in *what he does*. He, in fact, has been known to move in a subtracting fashion to get his children to trust in him. Oswald Chambers said, "When God is beginning to get satisfied with us He will impoverish everything in the nature of fictitious wealth, until we learn that all our fresh springs are in Him."

When God comes through, as he always will eventually, he will do so at his own will, on his own schedule, and for his own glory! His schedule may not fit ours, and our feelings, pride, and sense of time will suffer in the process. He does not choose to keep his saints out of trouble and sometimes chooses to allow them to suffer intensely for the carrying out of his redemptive processes.

When Shadrach, Meshach, and Abednego were hauled before the king and charged with refusing to bow down and worship the golden image, their reply was: "God whom we serve is able to deliver us from the burning fiery furnace, and he will deliver us out of thine hand, O King. . . . BUT IF NOT, be it known unto thee, O King, that we will not serve thy gods, nor worship the golden image which thou hast set up" (Dan. 3:17-18). What I want you to notice is the statement *"but if not."* They were ready for the but-if-nots. Suppose God does not deliver us or come through on our schedule. Will he cease to be God? Will I stop following him?

An old Quaker was heard talking to God in this manner, "God, I am not surprised that you have as few friends as you do because of the way you treat the ones you have!" There are times when that statement is encouraging. I thought that I was the only one who ever felt that way. Many have been the times when I wanted to say, "God, aren't you going to do something?"

I have gone out on a limb and made a statement that at first was probably unwelcome to you. I have said that there are times when God doesn't come through. Let us look at historical proof of the truth of this statement.

God did not come through to bring Moses out of the wilderness until after forty years.

God did not come through to release Samson from the Philistine prison.

God did not come through to keep Daniel out of the lion's den.

God did not come through to keep Jeremiah out of the dungeon.

God did not come through to keep Job out of the clutches of the devil.

God did not come through to save Naboth from a cruel death at the hands of Jezebel's henchmen.

God did not come through to keep Joseph from being sold into Egyptian slavery. Nor did he come through to discover the deceit of Potiphar's wife.

God did not come through to keep the three Hebrew children out of the fiery furnace.

God did not come through to preserve the life of John the Baptist. Instead his head was brought in on a platter to please a godless woman.

God did not come through for Paul to keep him from shipwreck, stoning, imprisonment, and finally martyrdom.

God did not come through to keep the authorities from banishing the apostle John to the Isle of Patmos.

In fact, it is obvious that from the human side God did not come through for Jesus to keep him from the cross. Instead he allowed him to suffer and die.

I believe that you must, by now, be getting what I am saying. There is a difference in God's *acts* and God's *ways*. The psalmist said that God made known his *ways* unto Moses and his *acts* unto the children of Israel. Many have been the times that he has chosen to delay his acts in order to install his ways. He may allow many to see his acts but he will entrust only to a few the knowledge of his ways. It has been the way of God many times to be still and silent in order to bring redemptive process to bear in the situation.

In most of the cases we have named when God did not come through, it would have been nothing short of a tragedy if he had come through!

There are three statements which are of considerable help to me. I mention them and briefly discuss them.

When God doesn't come through, *it is never because he is unable.* The three Hebrew children had settled upon one fact above all else. "Our God is able," they declared unto the king. When that matter is settled, we are settled. The condition of our hearts when we are in a strait, is greatly affected by our view of God. If he is not speaking or acting because he can't, then we have reason to worry. If it is because he can but won't for a purpose he doesn't care to divulge, then we can relax. God is able! There is tremendous consolation in knowing that he can.

When God doesn't come through, it is sometimes because *we are unprepared.* Time is a great problem to most of us, but a great tool for God. We think in terms of the "right nows," but God views the eternal perspective. Sometimes we need to spiritually soak before the Lord. The lesson, to be remembered, must be enforced by much time. Moses may need forty years on the "backside of nowhere" in order to prepare his heart to lead God's children out of Egypt. Not one moment of that time is wasted. When Joseph was prepared, he was elevated to be the prime minister of Egypt. It would have been tragic if the timing had been any other than what it was.

Finally, when God doesn't come through *it is always in order to work out his eternal redemptive purpose.* You have already seen the obvious. God's view of the eventual gives him the advantage of right timing. He did not deliver the three Hebrew children *from* the furnace at first because he wanted to deliver them *in* it. The greater glory came to him and the greater good came to them.

God did not come through to spring Paul from prison because he wanted the epistles written that were penned there.

God did not keep John the Beloved from Patmos Isle because he wanted Revelation written.

He did not take Jesus off the cross and heal his wounds because the death of Jesus was the only means of paying the debt of sin.

What about all the others we have not taken time to explain? They need no explanation because God can't be explained. Neither do his works need to be defended or justified. His ways are not up for vote. He works all things after the counsel of his own will.

Yes, there are times when God does not come through in our timing and yet he always will come through. We need to give him such a free hand with ourselves that he could mind his business in us in his own way and not ever hear a murmur from us.

8
Under the Juniper Tree

This chapter is prayerfully and respectfully dedicated to all the saints of God who have ever experienced discouragement in any form. I have repaired again and again to its truths to find again and again the delightful disciplines that result from obedience in times of distress.

JRT

We are never immune from the possibility of discouragement. In fact, in the midst of discouragement and antagonism God builds the strongest saints. Many of the psalms were written from a distressed heart. Of this the psalmist declared, "Thou hast enlarged me when I was in distress" (Ps. 4:1).

An allegorical story is told of a meeting of the devils of hell. It was a strategy session and the issue was how to defeat Christians in their daily living. The innovating emissaries of evil made many suggestions including casting suspicion on the Bible, the character of Christ, and the nature of God. They suggested outright persecution, gradual infiltration, and laws legislating religion. At last a bright young demon came up with an idea recognized by all to be the key. He suggested slowly planting bits of bad news here and there until discouragement had taken over. That was it! The devils would be trained in inducing discouragement.

Elijah was one of God's mightiest men! He stood up and out in the Old Testament like a granite wall for God. In obedience to God he walked into the palace one day and announced to King

Ahab that there would be neither dew nor rain for years until he gave the word. It did not rain for three and one half years! At the end of that period of time God commanded Elijah to show himself. Elijah found Ahab and Obadiah out searching for puddles of water for the livestock. Ahab exploded when he saw him. "Art thou he that troubleth Israel?", Ahab inquired. Elijah replied, "I have not troubled Israel; but you and your father's house in that you have forsaken the commandments of the Lord and followed after Baal" (See 1 Kings 18:17-18).

Elijah then proposed a massive confrontation with the people, the prophets of Baal, Ahab, and himself. They gathered on top of Mount Carmel. Altars were built and rules were drawn. Elijah was in full command! The *visible* contest was between Elijah and Jezebel's prophets, four hundred and fifty of Baal and four hundred of the groves. The *invisible* contest was between the hosts of hell and the God of heaven.

The issue was as fair as it was clear. "How long halt ye between two opinions? If the Lord be God, follow him: but if Baal, then follow him!" proposed Elijah. He further proposed that two altars be constructed, one for sacrificing to Baal and the other for sacrificing to God. He then challenged them: "Call ye on the name of your gods, and I will call upon the name of the Lord: AND THE GOD THAT ANSWERETH BY FIRE, LET HIM BE GOD" (1 Kings 18:24). The stage was set. All was ready! The altar to Baal was built. The bullock was prepared and now only the fire was lacking. Prayers to Baal were begun. Noon came and there was no answer. The Bible thoughtfully put it this way, "But there was no voice, nor any that answered."

Elijah, filled with confidence that Baal would not answer and equally as confident that his God would answer, taunted and teased the hapless prophets of Baal. "Cry aloud: for he is a god; either he is talking, or he is pursuing, or he is in a journey, or peradventure he sleepeth, and must be awaked" (1 Kings 18:27). The response of the prophets was violent exhibition. They cried and cut themselves with knives until blood gushed. This continued until the time of the evening sacrifice and still: "There was neither voice, nor any to answer, nor any that regarded."

In 1 Kings 18:30, we see Elijah confidently drawing the people close to watch what he does. He does three things. One looks *backward* and emphasizes REPAIR; one looks *forward* and emphasizes PREPARE; the other looks *upward* and emphasizes PRAYER. In other words the three things that always get God into action in any given situation are *correction* (repair), *anticipation* (prepare), and *supplication* (prayer).

Man can build his altars. He can build them into any shape or dimension. They may be large or small, impressive or simple. BUT ONLY GOD CAN SEND THE FIRE. Elijah evidenced ample anticipation when he prepared for the falling of the fire. The altar was repaired, the bullock was prepared, and water was poured upon the sacrifice, wood, and ground around the altar. He ordered the pouring of the water three times. He was absolutely certain of the outcome!

Then Elijah prayed a prayer that involved less than seventy words in the English narrative. And the record is, "Then the fire of the Lord fell, and consumed the burnt sacrifice, and the wood, and the stones, and the dust, and licked up the water that was in the trench" (1 Kings 18:38).

The people shouted, "The Lord, he is the God!" The Lord, he is the God!" The prophets of Baal were set upon and slain. What a day for the Lord God of Israel and his prophet, Elijah! The victory was complete. To add to the victory, Elijah announced that there would be a rain presently! The last verses of this vital, victorious chapter record, "There was a great rain . . . and the hand of the Lord was upon Elijah; and he girded up his loins and ran before Ahab to the entrance of Jezreel." Few days in history have recorded such resounding victories as this! My heart quickens as I recount this series of events.

But Then . . .

I have gone into some detail to show you that the preceding victories won on the field by Elijah were not cheap, shallow, or hollow. This was indeed a genuine uncontestable move of God. There is no way to impeach its genuineness. I want you to be ready for the "but thens." We are addressing ourselves to things that sometimes happen in or following a great and notable move of God's Spirit. The "but thens" are sometimes rather predictable. A new chain of events begins. You may begin to look for them . . . AFTER THE SPIRIT COMES!

To say the least, Ahab went home to the palace slightly upset. He was forced to report to Jezebel, his wife, the events of the day. Her prophets, who dined daily at her table, were slain with the sword and her cause was in reproach. She was violent with anger and promptly sent to Elijah a message that promised death within twenty-four hours (1 Kings 19:2). There begins here what I choose to call the *Juniper Tree Syndrome* or the *Post-Carmel Letdown*. It has or will happen to us all. We can and ought to be ready for it.

Elijah, the giant of Mount Carmel, in a matter of a few brief days is reduced to a cowering, crawling, cringing wretch pleading for a merciful death! He is UNDER THE JUNIPER TREE! I emphasize that location for a purpose. Remember it! You will be back here when the experience comes and will be more eager for the information given here than you are now. I want to make four basic statements which have been of inestimable help to me during these obviously unavoidable letdowns. If we are to go on in the Spirit, we must come to grips with the meaning of the spiritual "pit-stops" along the way. *Expectation with preparation* may mean the difference between victory and defeat.

Well, there's your hero and mine UNDER THE JUNIPER TREE! I almost titled this chapter WHAT'S A SPIRIT-FILLED PREACHER LIKE YOU DOING IN A PLACE LIKE THIS? Is this the same leather-lunged prophet that teased the enemy while outnumbered eight hundred and fifty to one? Is this the same mighty man who stood flat-footed and dressed down the king of the nation without batting an eye? Indeed it is! And you and I are not beyond the juniper tree experience either!

Four Basic Statements

Statement one: *Carelessness amid blessings can land you there . . . under the juniper tree.*

I may assume some things at this point but I believe them to be assumptions that are satisfyingly safe. There are three basic dangers that lurk in times of blessings. They are somewhat connected as relatives, one preparing for the other. The first of these is *preoccupa-*

tion. In times of spiritual blessings the pace is severely accelerated. Old disciplines are shaken and are apt to be left in the excitement of a new set of demands. It is obvious in the reading of the narrative of 1 Kings 19 that Elijah in his preoccupation forgot some things. When he received the threatening telegram from Jezebel, he could have nestled in the sweet memories of absolute provision and protection of Jehovah God in the past. What had he to be afraid of, really? Had not the very elements listened to his prophecy? Was not the rain withheld at his word? Had not God commandeered the ravens to bring his daily meals? Did not God provide for him through the widow at Zarephath? Did not God raise the widow's son from the dead? *Surely with that kind of backing he needed not to be afraid of a wicked woman!* Preoccupation with forgetfulness may have been the culprit.

The second danger is *presumption.* In times of spiritual excitement and effectiveness this is a common foe. The mighty moving of God came about through much prayer with repentance. It will continue only on the same basis. It is easy in times like these to presume that yesterday's brokenness is price enough for today's blessings. Not so! There must not be the slightest gap of presumption in the life that waits entirely on the Lord!

The third danger is *prayerlessness.* I can only assume that Elijah may have forgotten his prayer time that morning. I can more than assume, in fact I can assert, that he reacted without praying when he is pictured thusly, "And when he saw *that,* he arose and went for his life" (1 Kings 19:3). There is an unspoken tendency to believe that when things are going well and God is freely moving there is less need to pray than at other times. The exact opposite is true. Times of blessings are times of peril when prayer is desperately needed.

Statement two: *Inconsistencies abound there . . . under the juniper tree.*

Discouragement is never feasible. It is always based on false information or true information with severe leanings. It helps to face the farce of our discouragements. Martin Luther's wife, on one occasion, said to Luther, "Martin, I am sorry that your God is dead!" He quickly responded, "Why, God is not dead!" "You seem to be acting as discouraged as if HE was!" she observed. Sometimes wives have a gift of deromanticizing our discouragements. I remember on one occasion giving in to severe discouragement. I dramatically announced to my wife one day, "Honey, I am a total failure!" She was not impressed. Instead of sympathy, which I did not need, she matter-of-factly observed, "You know that may be some kind of record . . . a total failure at twenty-five!" I got the message!

Are you under the juniper tree? Have you given in to discouragement? If you are not careful, the added weight of self-disappointment will make the situation even more severe. I venture to suggest that some of the inconsistencies which abounded in Elijah's case may be evident in yours as well.

First, there is the inconsistency of *mistaken observations*. The Bible says, "When he saw THAT . . . he went for his life." What was the "that" which caused him to panic. He saw the threat of Jezebel, and immediately his thoughts must have gone haywire. How fertile can our imaginations become when for one moment we look to "that" instead of God. Elijah saw "that" when he should have riveted his vision upon the unswerving purpose and unchanging character of God. Never establish your direction on the basis of what others may present as a problem. We are not to base our goings or our stoppings on "that," whatever it may be!

Second, there is the inconsistency of *self-preservation*. The statement which characterized the escape of Elijah was, "and he went for his life." He made a decision based on the passion for self-preservation. This is always a mistake. God said to Jeremiah, "I am with thee to deliver thee, saith the Lord" (Jer. 1:8). Wherever God sends us he promises to guard us. That is all the protection we need and if we stop to defend ourselves we shall *dilute* our devotion.

Listen to what Oswald Chambers says, "The Sermon on the Mount indicates that when we are on Jesus Christ's errands, there is no time to stand up for ourselves. Jesus tells us in effect not to be bothered with whether you are being justly dealt with or not. To look for justice is a sign of deflection of devotion to Him. Never look for justice in this world, but never cease to give it. If we look for justice . . . we will begin to grouse and to indulge in the discontent of self-pity. If we are devoted to Jesus Christ we have nothing to do with what we meet, whether it is just or unjust. Jesus says, 'Go steadily on with what I have told you to do and I will guard your life.' IF YOU TRY TO GUARD YOURSELF, YOU REMOVE YOURSELF FROM MY DELIVERANCE!" Amen! One of Elijah's mistakes was that often indulged in by all of us . . . that of taking the safety of life into account. If we belong to God exclusively, the safety of our lives is exclusively his business.

Third, there is the inconsistency of *self-exaltation*. Now the truth surfaces as he confesses, "I am not better than my fathers!" What does that reveal? Simply that there was a time when he considered that he *was* better than his fathers. Many of us fall into the pitfall of thinking that just because God is using us in a signal manner that we are better than those whom he seems not to be using in the same measure of manifestation. It is easy indeed to assume that the blessings of the Lord in obvious abundance upon our ministry means that he has thought us better than others of his children. Not so!

Fourth, there is the inconsistency of *mistaken location*. When we run as a result of panic, we seldom run in the right direction. He went to Beersheba! What a place to go if he had in mind finding anyone who would be sympathetic with his situation. The king in Beersheba was none other than the son-in-law of Jezebel! Krummacher, in his well-written biography of Elijah says: "Instead of soaring above these threatenings as on eagles' wings, and looking down upon them in sublime composure, as on former occasions, the presence of human terror seems to have been too strong for his mind."

Do you see the inconsistency of it all? He takes the wrong things into account, moves to protect his life, then prays that God would take it! Had he really wanted to die he could have waited a few hours on Jezebel and she would have gladly accommodated him! And, by the way, he ran almost one hundred miles in the wrong direction. Discouraged folks are seldom good geographers.

Statement three: *Divine presence and provision meet us there . . . under the juniper tree.*

Now that we have nudged and elbowed our way through the negatives, let us come to the positives. The enemy will try to tell you that you are through when you awaken under the juniper tree. He will lead you to such self-disappointment that you will be led to believe that your usefulness is a thing of the past. Never believe the bad newscasts you hear while you are under the juniper tree. The devil has a viciously negative mind.

It is worth noticing that after the bitter complaint of Elijah in 1 Kings 19:4, God had not one word to say. Listen to the text of Elijah's declaration: "It is enough; now, O Lord, take away my life; for I am not better than my fathers." That statement would fall more in the category of a *burst of bitterness* than of a *statement of saneness*. How many times have we supposed ourselves to have advanced in maturity to such an extent that we were beyond much selfish whining only to discover a whole area of unsubmissive self-pity. God will go to almost any extreme to get us in circumstances so as to discover that part of our ego yet uncrucified and expose it to the killing rays of Calvary! Praise his name for this! As painful as this might be, glory waits around the corner.

I promised the positive and here it is! Speaking of glory . . . put your imagination to the scene which follows. God doesn't reply to the burst of bitterness and self-pity. He merely lets Elijah sleep. Have you discovered that there are times when the most spiritual thing to do is to take a nap? Fatigue is often the gateway to gloom and discouragement. Seldom does anything look right when we are weary physically. After the nap an angel comes. Feature the messenger of God coming through the awful wilderness and looking under the juniper tree. With a look half-amused and half-elated with his discovery, the angel sets to cooking supper. God has sent one of his special gourmet angels! Supper is finished and the angel nudges the overwrought prophet awake. He awakens and eats his supper in meditative silence only to go asleep again. Another nap and another meal and he is ready for his journey to meet God. Divine presence and provision have met Elijah . . . UNDER THE JUNIPER TREE.

Statement four: *Divine dynamic and direction escort us from there . . . under the juniper tree.*

Alas, our *disappointment* may be *his appointment!* We are not disqualified by discouragement. God has unfulfilled plans and he has counted us in on them. We may have hit bottom but he is not through! We may not understand the proceedings but then we are not called to understand . . . only obey.

After the journey from Beersheba and the juniper tree, Elijah lodged in a cave. The word of the Lord came to him and said,

"Elijah, what doest thou here?" Now, that is always a good question. It calls for present (and sometimes painful) evaluation. What are you doing here? That simple question cuts through complication and gets to the heart of the matter. Elijah's answer demonstrates the fact that he is not ready to give an answer. He is still having trouble with himself. He answers in a manner less than completely becoming. "I have been very jealous for the Lord God of hosts: for the children of Israel have forsaken thy covenant, thrown down thine altars, and slain thy prophets with the sword; and I, even I only, am left; and they seek my life, to take it away" (1 Kings 19:10).

Straightway, God commands Elijah to go and stand on the mount before the Lord. There God manifests his mighty power. An understanding of this episode may give us much information for times of spiritual upheaval. God caused a great wind which split the mountains and broke the rocks in pieces. But he was not in the wind. He sent an earthquake which caused the earth to quiver and shake, but he was not in the earthquake. He caused a fire, but he was not in the fire. He caused *all* of them, yet he was in *none* of them. Obviously here was a clear demonstration of the power and might of God. Here are all the qualities of an atom bomb . . . wind, earthquake, and fire. What is God saying through this awesome demonstration? Try this on for size:

Elijah, there's no power shortage with me. I have it all in my hand. If you are trying to protect me, you can relax . . . I can take care of myself. But even in view of these manifestations of my might I had rather you yield to my *message* than worship my *might*.

We have a problem today . . . so many folks are wanting to start movements around the wind, the earthquake, and the fire. While God may use these to command our attention, he still speaks with a still, small voice! I believe I'll keep my membership in the *First Church of the Still Small Voice!*

After the dynamic demonstration, God asks the same question and receives the same answer. I am not sure that Elijah understood the situation at that point, but I have a feeling that though his answer was word for word the same as before his spirit was subdued and submissive. The *dynamic* having been presented . . . the *direction* awaits. The directions God gives almost make one dizzy! Hours ago

Elijah had stood at the point which he believed marked the end of his ministry. Now, he could hardly believe his ears. What is God saying?

> Lord, you couldn't be talking to me,
> I've just been under the juniper tree!
> I've been discouraged, defeated, you see . . .
> I'm sure you couldn't be talking to me!
> Lord, what's this you're saying to me?
> Go crown two kings as quick as can be . . .
> And anoint a young prophet to minister with me?
> You say there are 7,000 with unbended knee?
> Lord, I must have been wrong for it looks like to me
> That the best of my ministry is just yet to be!
> So forgive my indulgent distress and self-pity spree . . .
> And from here . . . let all of my springs be discovered in thee!

Praise God, he does not abandon us under the juniper tree! Elijah goes from there to the greatest days of his glorious ministry! Your discouragement and mine is not a deadend but just a turn in the road! There are kings to *crown*, enemies to *conquer*, and prophets to *call*. Be about it! These are the greatest days yet and they precede still greater days.

Discouragement, whatever its reason, has been a discipline! Lift up your head with me . . . the best is yet to be! Elijah, you have heard the still small voice . . . the gentle whisper of gospel grace. Be about it now! His strength is made perfect in your weakness! How can we be discouraged with our weakness when it is the necessary platform for his mighty strength?

Somehow the psalmist's doxology is fitting here:

> Lift up your heads, O ye gates; and be ye lift up ye everlasting doors; and the King of glory shall come in. Who is this King of glory? The Lord, strong and mighty, the Lord mighty in battle. Lift up your heads, O ye gates; even lift them up, ye everlasting doors; and the King of glory shall come in. Who is this King of glory? The Lord of hosts, he is the King of glory (Ps. 24:7-10).

Have you taken up residence . . . under the juniper tree? Would you just join me in repeating the four statements which we have rehearsed here?

Statement one:	*Carelessness amid blessings may land you there . . . under the juniper tree.*
Statement two:	*Inconsistencies abound there . . . under the juniper tree.*
Statement three:	*Divine presence and provision meet us there . . . under the juniper tree.*
Statement four:	*Divine dynamic and direction escort us from there . . . under the juniper tree.*

Would you now implore God to move you from *JUNIPER TREE ALLEY* to *MOUNT HOREB BOULEVARD* and then on to *FULNESS FREEWAY?*

May I tell how I know that it will work? I began this chapter under the juniper tree. The information herein recounted has been used by the Spirit and has brought me out. Through discouragement come new discoveries and delights!

9
Shields of Brass for Shields of Gold

In the midst of mighty moves of God in history a testimony is given. Those testimonies shine like the shields of gold fashioned by Solomon of old. We must always be on guard lest the enemy steal away our testimonies as did Shishak. Once robbed of our former glory we face two alternatives. We may storm the enemy and win back our victory, or we may substitute the good and glittering for the gold and glory.

JRT

"And he took away the treasures of the house of the Lord, and the treasures of the king's house; he even took away all; and he took away all the shields of gold which Solomon had made. And King Rehoboam made in their stead brasen shields, and committed them unto the hands of the chief of the guard, which kept the door of the king's house" (1 Kings 14:26-27).

Solomon's Splendor

The glory of Solomon's kingdom was almost beyond the wildest imaginations even in view of today's measurements. Solomon asked for wisdom and God gave him both wisdom and wealth. The endeavor for which Solomon is best known was the building of the great Temple. No building in antiquity or since can compare with this Temple. The Illinois Society of Architects in 1925 set out to make estimates of the cost of rebuilding the Temple. The cost of the building alone, without the vessels, the trumpets, the priests' vestments, and other furnishings was estimated at *eighty-seven billion dollars!* It was conservatively estimated that building costs doubled between 1925 and 1961 when the report was given. Of course building costs have skyrocketed during the past few years. There is little doubt but that the Temple of Solomon today would cost in excess of *five hundred billion dollars*.

And the Temple was only a part of the overall wealth of the kingdom headed by Solomon. His great wealth is described in part in the book of Ecclesiastes as he reports: "I made me great works; I builded me houses; I planted me vineyards: I made me gardens and orchards, and I planted trees in them of all kinds of fruit: I made me pools of water, to water therewith the wood that bringeth forth trees: I got me servants and maidens and had servants born in my house; also I had great possessions of great and small cattle above all that were in Jerusalem before me; I gathered me silver and gold, and the peculiar treasures of kings and of the provinces: I got me men singers and women singers, and the delights of the sons of men, as musical instruments, and that of all sorts. *So I was great,* increased more than all that were before me in Jerusalem: also my wisdom remained with me. AND WHATSOEVER MINE EYES DESIRED I KEPT NOT FROM THEM, I WITHHELD NOT MY HEART FROM ANY JOY; FOR MY HEART REJOICED IN ALL MY LABOUR: AND THIS WAS MY PORTION OF ALL MY LABOUR" (Eccl. 2:4-10).

The glory of the kingdom and the greatness of the king were signs of the approval of God upon the nation. The reign of Solomon, at least in the initial stages, could be looked upon as a time of revival. Doubtless if Solomon could have been gauged in New Testament measurements he would have been labeled as a Spirit-filled and Spirit-anointed man. He moved in the wisdom of God and in the power of God. The kingdom was a wonder and a marvel to all the kingdoms round about. Folks came from all over the world in absolute awe to behold the glory of Solomon's kingdom. The Queen of Sheba came to see and remarked before she left: "Howbeit I believed not the words, until I came and mine eyes have seen it; and behold, the half was not told me; thy wisdom and prosperity exceedeth the fame which I heard." The significant thing about the wealth and wisdom of Solomon was that it caused the heathen around them to bless the Lord. Listen to the response of the Queen of Sheba: "Blessed be the Lord thy God, which delighteth in thee, to set thee on the throne of Israel: because the Lord loved Israel for ever, therefore made he thee King, to do justice and judgement" (1 Kings 10:9).

There has surely never been a season in history when so much power was exerted by one man as in the days of Solomon. His power was evident in every realm of life. He had intellectual power, having asked God for wisdom. He had spiritual power, having this record, "And Solomon loved the Lord, walking in the statutes of David his father" (1 Kings 3:3).

Listen to a later description of Solomon: "And God gave Solomon wisdom and understanding exceeding much, and largeness of heart, even as the sand that is on the sea shore. And Solomon's wisdom excelled the wisdom of all the children of the east country, and all the wisdom of Egypt. For he was wiser than all men" (1 Kings 4:29-31). And in another place it is said: "So Solomon exceeded all the kings of the earth for riches and for wisdom. And all the earth sought to Solomon, to hear his wisdom, which God had put in his heart" (1 Kings 10:23-24).

Because of the moving of God to grant Solomon such capacities, there was spiritual, moral, economic, intellectual, and military greatness not known before and possibly since!

The Symbolism of the Shields

During the magnificent reign of Solomon, hundreds of traditions were established which were intended as manifestations of the glory of the kingdom. It is recorded that Solomon made three hundred shields of beaten gold (1 Kings 10:17). Each shield contained three pounds of gold. Each shield was a gleaming testimony of the greatness of the king and his kingdom. Can you imagine the imposing sight that met the visitor as men bearing the golden shields lined the pathway to the king's dwelling? For more than the length of a modern football field the shields lined the path along which the visitor walked or rode. The shields reflected the sun's rays sending gleaming reflections across the countryside.

Those gleaming golden shields were at once the symbol of the purity and integrity of the nation and its leadership. They were reminders of the glory of Jehovah God and the greatness of his blessings upon the nation. They were testimonies of the approval of God and the thanksgiving of the people for their covenant relationship with the God of heaven.

These shields may well have been used in worship services to glorify the name of God. They may have been so large that a man could stand behind one of them and hide himself entirely. Here was a picture of a man covered by the blessing of God. Thus, the shields of gold became worldwide symbols of the splendor and power of one nation under God.

Shields of the Spirit Today

Today God in his infinite wisdom and limitless wealth has given to us some golden shields. Born in the glorious era which first marked the moving of the Spirit of God in this dispensation, the church has lined the path of history with those golden shields. They are shields of peerless gold mined in the depths of men's commitment to God and God's commitment to men. There are shields of persistency and power; of conviction and consecration; of selflessness and sacrifice; of moral and spiritual strength.

We who live in the fading years of the twentieth century have seen a move of God. In the early seventies there were notable spiritual breakthroughs everywhere, accompanied by immediate repentance and spontaneous joy. Testimonies came out of great movings of the Spirit of God. The Asbury Awakening of 1970, breakthroughs in South America, revival in Indonesia, and great harvests in Korea characterize the seventies.

God seemed to wait until the "God-is-dead" crowd finished its investigations and launched the campaign aimed at notifying the world that the God of heaven had long since expired. Then he moved . . . mightily and marvelously! In cold, dry churches across the land he moved. Unexcited shepherds were set aflame in their pulpits and the flames spread. Movements intended to implement the dynamic and design of revival were born. Laymen began to take their place in the spiritual hedges and manifested their willingness to stand in the gaps before God in the land. A new hunger has come to the land of the free and the home of the brave! Doubtless we have seen a time of the moving of God. Never has there been more talk of the Holy Spirit since Pentecost! Never has there been more openness to real desires of God for his people.

But in times like these there are dangers always lurking. The days which marked the closing of Solomon's reign and the beginning of Rehoboam's reign have some vital lessons for us today.

Stolen Shields

God had promised Solomon: "And if thou wilt walk before me, as David thy father walked, in integrity of heart, and in uprightness, to do according to all that I have commanded thee, and wilt keep my statutes and my judgements: then will I establish the throne of thy kingdom upon Israel for ever, as I promised to David thy father, saying, There shall not fail thee a man upon the throne of Israel" (1 Kings 9:4-5).

God's promise, however, was followed by a threat: "But if ye shall turn at all from following me, ye or your children, and will not keep my commandments and my statutes which I have set before you, but go and serve other gods, and worship them; THEN WILL I CUT OFF ISRAEL OUT OF THE LAND WHICH I HAVE GIVEN THEM: AND THIS HOUSE, WHICH I HAVE HALLOWED FOR MY NAME, WILL I CAST OUT OF MY SIGHT: AND ISRAEL SHALL BE A PROVERB AND A BYWORD AMONG ALL THE PEOPLE" (1 Kings 9:6-7).

Then the sad record is that "Solomon loved many strange women. . . . Of the nations concerning which the Lord said unto the children of Israel. Ye shall not go in to them, neither shall they come in unto you: for surely they will turn away your heart after their gods" (1 Kings 11:1-2). And it was as the Lord had warned: "For it came to pass, when Solomon was old, that his wives turned away his heart after other gods: and his heart was not perfect with the Lord his God, as was the heart of David his father. . . . And Solomon did evil in the sight of the Lord" (1 Kings 11:4,6).

The glory waned and the greatness wilted. The kingdom was soon divided. The enemies around them were stirred against them. Rehoboam, Solomon's son, succeeded his father after he died. He continued in idolatrous ways, listening to the bad advice of young men to put a heavier yoke upon the people. Tragedy struck again and again. Death came to the king's house and he sadly buried his son. Abominations came to the land in multitudes. The Word sums it up by saying, "And Judah did evil in the sight of the Lord, and they provoked him to jealousy with their sins which they had committed, above all that their father had done" (1 Kings 14:22).

The weakened nation was prey for all the nations around it. After five years under the reign of Rehoboam, Shishak, the king of Egypt, came against Jerusalem. In an act of sheer arrogance Shishak stole the treasures from the king's house. Specific mention is made of the shields of gold. "He took away all the shields of gold which Solomon had made" (1 Kings 14:26). This seemed to stand as the crowning blow that indicated the depths of shame to which the nation had sunk. Now, the testimony was gone. The glory had departed.

Substitute Shields

Strangely enough the last recorded act of Rehoboam in 1 Kings was the substitution of brass shields for the stolen golden shields. It may well have been the act which best described the whole character of this weak and wicked king. Recognizing that the golden shields were gone, he faced a decision. He could storm the enemy's strongholds and retrieve the precious golden shields or he could effect a compromise. The value of the shields of gold was impressive enough . . . in today's values they would be worth more than two million dollars. Their spiritual and symbolic worth was much more significant. The fact was that Rehoboam recognized his nation's weakness to be such that he probably couldn't win a battle with Egypt.

So Rehoboam compromised! He made brass likenesses of the real golden shields. The new shields at best were rather cheap imitations of the real thing. Rehoboam was both unwilling to live for a great cause or die for a great ideal. He would not take the risk! He would not buck the crowd. He would not fight for anything. Thus, the last recorded act of Rehoboam was to compromise! *He had substituted shields of brass for shields of gold.*

Similar Situations Today

What happened to Rehoboam may happen in the spiritual realm today. Those brass shields became a reminder of God's blessings sacrificed for convenience. They told of the glory of a former day and the loss of that glory.

Vance Havner says, "We often see the spiritual counterpart in

Christian experience. Satan steals our shields of gold and we try to cover our defeat and hide our chagrin by making in their stead shields of brass!

"At Pentecost the church began with shields of gold. But that which began in the Spirit tried later to make itself perfect in the flesh. Constantine embraced Christianity and the church joined hands with the world. Harnack tells us, 'As the proofs of the Spirit and of power subsided after the beginning of the third century, the extraordinary moral tension also became relaxed, paving the way gradually for a morality which was adapted to a worldly life.' "

"The church began to compromise, so as to be less offensive to an ungodly age. When Thomas Aquinas visited the Pope and was being shown the splendor of the papal treasures, the pontiff remarked, 'You will observe that the church no longer has to say, 'silver and gold have I none.' And Aquinas answered, 'Neither can she say 'Rise up and walk.' Shishak has stolen the shields of gold and men were substituting shields of brass." [1]

This is an old game with the devil . . . substituting the good for the best. And we are still falling for the same old trick. We can have a brass relationship, a brass revival, a brass gift, a brass experience, a brass discipline. It may glitter and be impressive but it will soon turn dull with time.

In times of revival the danger is real that the devil will steal away the genuineness of what God has done when we get our eyes on human factors. It is a sad commentary on the spiritual state of affairs when we realize our losses and compromise instead of repent. These losses have occurred so slowly that we have not noticed until we have been slammed right up against the conditions of former days and see how far we have gone backward! It is sadder still when, having recognized the loss, we frantically step up activity, and build brass shields to replace the golden ones.

Preoccupied with the sensual enjoyments of revival we may recognize that the enemy has stolen the reality of spiritual blessedness. Repentance in times like these seems to come harder than in the days when revival began. It is much easier to fabricate experiences, counterfeit gifts, and contrive special "providences" to brace up our ailing faith. *Feeling* is substituted for faith and signs are substituted for genuine spiritual life. We may find ourselves holding shields of brass instead of shields of gold.

Do you find yourself with the shield of *human effort* substituted for the shield of divine *energy*, of *carnality* for *commitment*, of *program* for *power*, of *apathy* for *abandonment*, of *compromise* for *consecration?*

What do you do then? When the sickening realization that two evils have been committed . . . what then? We may have been the victims of an inglorious theft . . . our golden shields have been taken! We may have worsened the situation by substituting the less expensive through compromise. What then?

Bombard heaven with confessions of the compromise! Regain those positions where folks give all in order to take all. Tell God you want back those shields of gold at any cost. Storm the strongholds of hell and do not leave until the treasures of the king's house are brought back! Anything less than *all* that God gives is a shield of brass. Be done with it!

Let it not be written of any of us that we were guilty in the midst of these dramatic days of substituting *shields of brass for shields of gold!*

10
The
Rod
of God

"There is a shortage of 'going on' truth. There is a principle written within the narrative covering the first five verses of Exodus 4 which would give continuation to the victory of many a saint. The 'going on' truth therein is indispensable to the overcomer.

JRT

"And thou shalt take this rod in thine hand, wherewith thou shalt do signs" (Ex. 4:17).

"And Moses took the rod of God in his hand" (Ex. 4:20).

After the Spirit comes there is the problem of continuing. Nowhere in the Bible is the principle of continuing made any clearer than in the ministry of Moses. The pivot around which the principle revolves is the rod discussed in Exodus 4. The story of Moses is an exciting and meaningful one. It is freighted with spiritual significance for the pilgrim today. I can guarantee you that the principle contained within the framework of Exodus 4:1-5 will change your life so that it can never again be the same.

Beginning Right . . . Beginning Wrong

The life of Moses began right . . . with a miracle. You will remember that Moses was born during a time when boy babies were not winning any popularity contests. King Pharoah of Egypt was worried about the population explosion of the Hebrews and masterminded a scheme to decimate the population by killing all the boy babies. The midwives of Egypt cooperated with the Hebrews and saved many of the baby boys. The mother of Moses hid her baby boy in a little waterproof basket among the bullrushes of the river. It was here that the daughter of Pharoah came to bathe and found the baby. Seeing that he was a proper child, she took him to the palace to raise him. The sister of Moses was on guard when the baby was found and through the providence of God his mother was conscripted to be his nurse. So the lad grew up under palace auspices with the advantage of palace education, palace persuasion, palace influence, and palace finery. At the same time he had the advantage of the influence of his very own mother and he doubtlessly grew up knowing who he was and whose he was.

The record is written in Hebrews 11:24-26: "By faith Moses, when he was come to years, refused to be called the son of Pharoah's daughter; choosing rather to suffer affliction with the people of God, than to enjoy the pleasures of sin for a season; esteeming the reproach of Christ greater riches than the treasures of Egypt: . . . for he endured, as seeing him who is invisible."

Though the beginning of Moses' life was right, the beginning of his ministry was wrong. Let us recount the story of his abortive ministry. When Moses came of years, which was forty years of age, he went out unto his brethren. He saw an Egyptian mistreating one of his brethren. He looked this way and that way and saw nobody. He then proceeded to kill the Egyptian and hide him in the sand. This was the first day of his ministry. Now there is no one who can deny the commitment of Moses to the cause of freeing the Hebrews from the slavery of Egypt. His manner of going about what he felt called to do is another matter. He killed one Egyptian the first day! He did do something. We must give him some credit! However, it would have taken many years to weaken the structure of Egypt in this manner.

The second day of the ministry of Moses finds him about to negotiate a squabble between two Israelites. As he suggests that he might be of help, one of the Israelites reveals knowledge that he has of the episode the day before. He asked, "Do you intend to kill me as you killed the Egyptian?" (See Ex. 2:14). Moses feared that the matter was known and he was right. Pharoah heard and sought to slay Moses. Moses fled to the land of Midian where he was to spend the next forty years of his life. What a waste! Here was a man who had the finest education, the finest connections, the finest personality, and the finest background to equip him to be the deliverer of the children of Israel. And here he wasted his life for forty years. Was it wasted? It indeed turned out that God was shaping Moses to be the redeemer of God's children.

Why had the ministry failed? Were Moses' intentions not proper? I think they were. Was his commitment faulty? I think not. Was he not qualified? Did he not have enough education? I think it was neither of these. I think it was that he sought to do the job for God in his own strength. There is a vast difference between a man doing his best for God and God doing for his glory his normal in a man. Moses set out to do the work of God in the energy of his own flesh and the wisdom of his own intellect. The work of God is not done that way. *Perhaps the greatest weakness of Moses was his strength!* He had too much on the ball! Too much influence in high places was his. He had too much ability to encourage him to do the job himself. He had too many reasons to expect success to succeed in God's way. God's strength is made perfect in man's weakness. *Moses was simply not weak enough!* Many a man is too strong at first for God to use him in God's own way. There must first come a breaking in which a man learns to find all his strength in Jehovah God.

For forty years Moses learned to trust in God. He faced the nothingness of the flesh for forty years. He had forty years to brood over his abortive ministry until he was content with accepting the fact that he was worth no more than to spend the rest of his life herding a crowd of stupid sheep!

After forty years on the backside of the desert, the call of God came to Moses through a burning bush. God spoke in certain terms regarding the future deliverance of his children from Egyptian slavery. After a lengthy dialogue between Moses and God, they came to the confrontation recorded in Exodus 4.

I have been quite mystified with this passage for years. For most of that time I suppose that I believed that it simply marked a case of God showing in visual terms the greatness of his power in order to encourage Moses to go on. When I began to see that there was much more to it than this I began to look more closely into the circumstances surrounding that mysterious rod.

After God's call was made clear to Moses in Exodus 3, chapter four opens with Moses seeking to excuse himself thusly: "They will not believe me nor hearken to my voice: for they will say, The Lord hath not appeared unto thee." The confidence that Moses had in his own ability had greatly depreciated during those forty years in the wilderness! And did not he voice a fear which has lurked in all our hearts at one time or another? He feared that the people would not listen and heed, saying that his experience was not valid. He feared that he might go about doing the job as before without the credential of God's power. He simply would not go that route again!

Then God did something very strange. He asked Moses a question. "What is that in thine hand?" He queries. "Lord, it is a rod." "Cast it on the ground!"

And he cast it on the ground and it became a serpent and Moses ran from it. It was then that the Lord said, "Moses, pick it up by the tail." Whereupon he picked it up and it became a rod again in his hand.

The reason? "That they may believe that the Lord God of . . . Abraham, the God of Isaac, and the God of Jacob, hath appeared unto thee" (Ex. 4:5).

What a mysterious passage and what a mysterious experience! And yet there is a principle barely beneath the surface of this simple story which is the key to victory and the key to continuing. The whole principle revolves around the rod of Moses.

I believe that sanctified imagination is of great help in reading and teaching the Word of God. I do not have to imagine much to suspicion that there might well have been more to the conversation than is recorded in chapter four! I find it amusing to imagine that Moses was rather hesitant about the whole matter.

"Lord, you know what this is in my hand! It is a rod! It is a tool of the trade! A perfectly good rod at that, Lord.

"You say throw it down? Why should I? There is nothing wrong with this rod. It never did me any harm. It has helped me over uneven paths, equalized me against wild beasts, and has been my constant companion for years. I am not sure that I could do without it!

"Well, if you insist, but I'll have you know that I don't understand at all but here goes!

"Lord, that's a snake! I'll see you around! (Exit Moses!)

"What's that you say, Lord? Pick it up? By the tail? Lord I don't mean to be running your business, but if I pick this snake up by the tail what will happen to his business end?

"All right, Lord, whatever you say! Here goes!"

Then presently Moses stood as he had before with the rod in his hand but the whole face of the situation had changed. Something had happened. Moses was the same man with the same rod in his hand but relationships had been altered.

A while ago here was a man with a rod in his hand. God entered the picture and ordered the man to throw the rod down. It was done and then God gave the order to pick the snake up by the tail, which he did. It immediately turned again into a rod. *The snake was out and God was in!* Now here was a man with a rod in his hand but it was not his rod. It was God's! Before it could do only what a man could do. Now, it could do all that the God of heaven could do. Here was the best instance in the Old Testament of the New Testament experience of being filled with the Spirit. Here a man became the exclusive property of God. Moses belonged to God and the rod belonged to God. Up until now Moses had accomplished no miracles for he could only do what a man doing his best could do. That may be impressive and even moving but it is not miraculous! It is not enough merely to get the job done that God has called us to do.

There are two hints within Exodus 4 that lead us to believe that we have not seen the rod for the last time. In verse 17 we read, "And thou shalt take this rod . . . wherewith thou shalt do signs." Before it was "a rod" but now it is *"this* rod." Rods are a dime a dozen. What is it that takes "a" rod and makes it a specifically designated rod . . . "this" rod? The other verse may hold the answer. "And Moses took the *rod of God* in his hand" (Ex. 4:20). In the process somewhere, the *rod of a man* has become the *rod of God.* Before it was a simple rod in the hand of a simple man who had a desire to do something for God but had miserably failed. Now it is the rod of God in the hand of a man who has made himself available to God to do the work of God.

I am going to present seven propositions which I believe to be tremendously important as we consider events surrounding this mighty move of God.

Proposition one: *God always begins with us where we are and with what we have in our hands.*

He calls upon us to assess our present spiritual condition. It is not a matter of where we have been or where we hope one day to be. The "is" of our spiritual condition is all-important.

What is that in thine hand? Is it a plan of strategy? Is it an education or a key position? Is it a pastime or a sport? Is it an accomplishment or a great ability? It may be good in our eyes or bad in our eyes. God waits for the answer. It isn't because he doesn't know but because we need the experience of relating it. What is it? Something or someone you love very much? And you simply cannot fathom why God should require you to cast it down on the ground. After all it has done you no harm. It has been a thing of advantage.

But you throw it down and it becomes a serpent! Why? Read on!

Proposition two: *There is something of the nature of the serpent about anything that has not been thrown down and become God's exclusive property.*

Can you imagine Moses coming back to the place from which he had fled a few moments before only to find the deadly serpent still there! How could this have been his companion day after day for years? It had that deadly nature because it belonged to Moses and not God. The nature of the snake is the nature of self. Many a preacher, singer, or religious worker has worked for God doing their best, but never becoming God's property, only to find later that they had held a deadly serpent to their bosom. They worked well for God. They preached great sermons and the people were impressed. There voices rang to the thrill of thousands but self was still alive like a coiled serpent waiting to sink its deadly fangs into the testimony of the Lord and put it to death. Whatever you have in your hand, regardless of its seeming nature, there is a snake in it if it still belongs to you!

When Moses obeys and throws the rod on the ground the serpent is exposed. When Moses obeys and picks up the rod the serpent is removed.

In what relationship, gift, ability, talent, plan, proposal, profession, or connection is lurking the terrible enemy of self waiting to rise to reign?

Proposition three: Once it has become God's property he has the prerogative to return it if he wishes.

God is not interested in taking things away from us. He is interested in working in our lives with those things and using them to his glory in his power! The order to throw it down may be followed hard upon by the order to pick it up. It may sound as if God cannot make up his mind. But he knows perfectly well what he is doing. There is nothing wrong with the rod of Moses except that it is the rod of Moses. As long as it is the rod of Moses, it can never do anything more than the man Moses can do. But when it becomes God's property God's power comes into play. Now that Moses has obeyed, God can commit himself to Moses as he never has before.

"Pick it up Moses . . . by the tail."

Proposition four: *When we pick up that which has become God's property we always hold it lightly by the lesser end.*

It is now the *rod of God*. Now self has departed from it and God is in it! But beware and know that it is ours only as it is God's and as long as we recognize that it is his. He recognizes that it is ours. The business end of it is ever and always God's!

Proposition five: *From that point we can expect the results to manifest the works of God.*

Up until now the rod had accomplished no miracles. It was not the rod of God but the rod of a man. God declared, "Thou shalt take this rod in thine hand wherewith thou shalt do signs [miracles]" (Ex. 4:17). And it was so. The power of God upon Moses and his brother is symbolized in the rods in their hands. Through the rods, the plagues were called upon Egypt and with each plague a death blow was dealt to a section of Egyptian theology. The power of God had taken the field and nothing could stand! It was the work of God! It cannot and could not be explained! Man's work is predictable and explainable! Not so with God's!

Proposition six: *The key to continuing with God is the use of the rod.*

Being endued with power from on high does not mean that we will have a trouble-free existence from now on. For the first time

God can trust us with problems! And he will! I want you to notice three specific instances in which Moses faced problems with the rod being the key.

The *first crisis* was at the Red Sea. Here is the picture: There is a geographical barrier, a great multitude of people, a rapidly-approaching army, and a very nervous leader. The people begin to murmur. Their leader, Moses, begins to seek to comfort them saying: "Fear ye not, stand still, and see the salvation of the Lord, which he will show to you to day" (Ex. 14:13).

After his little speech Moses then obviously retires to a rather urgent prayer meeting. Permit me to imagine the conversation between God and Moses.

MOSES: "Lord, we have this terrible problem. You got us into this . . . now get us out!"

GOD: "Moses, what is that in thine hand?"

MOSES: "A rod, Lord, why do you ask?"

GOD: "A rod?"

MOSES: "Well, your rod, Lord!"

GOD: "What does it mean, Moses?"

MOSES: "Well, it means that I am yours and not mine and this rod is yours and not mine."

GOD: "And what else?"

MOSES: "Well, that congregation of griping people are not my problem, they are yours, Lord."

GOD: "And what else?"

MOSES: "Well, it means that the Red Sea is not mine; it is the Lord's problem too . . . and for that matter the whole situation is his."

GOD: "Now, Moses what was your problem?"

MOSES: "I guess, Lord, that I just didn't have a problem . . . just an opportunity!"

GOD: "Now, Moses quit crying to me and go forward!"

MOSES: "But Lord, there is a sea right out in front of us!"

GOD: "Yes, I know, but just stretch the rod out toward the sea and divide the sea."

That rod is emblematic of the power of a life which depends on God. It is a symbol of a Spirit-anointed life.

Moses does as God commands and the waters roll up on either

side and the people of God go across on dry land. Then Moses notices that Pharoah's army is using the same route.

MOSES: "Lord, here comes Pharoah's army. I think we may have forgotten something."

GOD: "No, Moses, I have thought of everything. What is that in your hand? My rod! Hold it over the sea!"

And as quickly as it was opened the sea is closed by an act of God. What had been the salvation of the people of God now becomes judgment upon God's enemies.

The fullness of the Spirit will liberate you from bondage.

The *second crisis* takes place in Exodus 17. God's people have run out of water. Their memory is short. They have forgotten the deliverance of the Lord back at the Red Sea. They murmur and threaten. And for a moment Moses forgets, too. He is heard to say: "Lord, what shall I do unto this people? They be almost ready to stone me" (Ex. 17:4). Who was it that told me that there were no problems in the walk with God?

The people had quickly forgotten miracle number one and two at the Red Sea and now they join in a chorus of complaining. As Moses talks to God he finds no panic in heaven. God is neither shocked nor disappointed but moves right ahead to show Moses the way. "And the Lord said to Moses, Go on before the people, and take with thee of the elders of Israel; AND THY ROD, wherewith thou smotest the river, take in thine hand, and go" (Ex. 17:5). There's the rod again! Do you remember what it symbolizes? It stands for a relationship with God in which God has control. It suggests the power of a God-anointed life, the Spirit-filled life, a life sold out to God. And God thoughtfully says, "Don't forget the rod!" Here is the key to continuing: REMEMBER THE ROD! Remember that it must not be by human might or by human power but by the Spirit of God!

God brings Moses and the elders to the rock in Horeb and orders him to smite the rock with the rod. I can easily imagine that if there is any humanity in Moses as there is in me, he would have entertained some question. "Lord, are you sure you know what you are asking me to do?" Looking at the matter from the human side left Moses with a muddled mind. But you see, since the rod of a man became the rod of God and the man became a man of God, he never will need to look at matters purely from the human side. God is in it with him! Do not forget that the rod in the hand of a man who is sold out to God can do more than a man can do . . . it can, in fact, do all that the God of heaven can do. Moses could have banged around on that old rock all day long and would have netted nothing but a bruised hand and a discouraged heart. But here he stands with the rod of God in his hand. In obedience to God he strikes the rock and the old rock splits wide open and a river gushes forth! Hallelujah!

The fullness of the Spirit will supply your every need!

You see, the same principle that delivered them from the clutches of Egypt's Pharoah and destroyed Pharoah's army is the principle that worked here at Horeb to slack their thirst and meet their needs.

The *third crisis* is found in the same chapter, Exodus 17:8. The first great problem was an *obstacle*, the river; the second problem was a *deficiency*, they were out of water; now the third problem was *opposition*, Amalek came to fight with Israel.

These problems are probably a representative cross section of the kinds of situations folks who follow the Lord will face!

Well, will it work when opposition comes? This time Moses doesn't need to be reminded! Listen to the narrative: "Then came Amalek, and fought with Israel in Rephidim. And Moses said to Joshua, Choose us out men, and go out, fight with Amalek; TO MORROW I WILL STAND ON THE TOP OF THE HILL *WITH THE ROD OF GOD IN MINE HAND*" (Ex. 17:8-9). "What do you expect this strategy to accomplish, Moses?" Praise the Lord, what worked on the problem of the Red Sea and on the rock at Horeb will work on old Amalek as well!

Now, if you miss every other truth in this chapter I want you to get this next truth firmly fixed in your mind and heart. It will save you from many a heartache. "AND IT CAME TO PASS, WHEN MOSES HELD UP HIS HAND, THAT ISRAEL PREVAILED: AND WHEN HE LET DOWN HIS HAND, AMALEK PREVAILED" (Ex. 17:11).

The principle of continuing is wrapped up in commitment to the fact that when the situation is wholly in God's hands there will be victory. When Moses held up the rod (a symbol of total reliance on God), Joshua was empowered to whip Amalek but when Moses let the rod down the battle tide turned. It will be so in your life and mine. When the rod of Spirit-fulness is lifted high, there is victory but when we relax for a moment and give in to prayerlessness, pride, or preoccupation we will lose the battle.

Aaron and Hur are with Moses on the mount and it doesn't take long for them to get the picture. Every time Moses lets down the rod the enemy prevails. Everytime he lifts it up Joshua prevails. They behold the importance of the uplifted rod! Listen to the thoughtful narrative: "But Moses hands were heavy; and they took a stone, and put it under him, and he sat thereon; AND AARON AND HUR STAYED UP HIS HANDS, the one on one side and the other on the other side; and his hands were steady until the going down of the sun" (Ex. 17:12).

There are many times when we can help each other in the matter of keeping on. God alone knows the importance of intercession in our experience. We need to help each other remember the rod and hold it up continually.

The result? The same as before! "And Joshua discomfited Amalek and his people with the edge of the sword" (Ex. 17:13).

The fulness of the Spirit will stop your enemies!

Resounding victory resulted! The name of God was glorified. They built an altar in the place of victory and called it "Jehovah-nissi" . . . GOD, OUR BANNER OF VICTORY. Conquest over the enemy was complete and Amalek was finished!

Now let's summarize! The ROD OF GOD symbolizes the POWER OF GOD upon the MAN OF GOD who will rely with all his life upon God. To hold it up meant the employment of the principle of God's power upon the situation. What worked in one situation worked in another and then another. The rod held high was a testimony of reliance on Jehovah God . . . at once a prayer and a confession of victory.

Moses held it up and the sea opened. He held it up again and the sea was closed drowning the enemy. He used it to smite the rock and water aplenty came out for everyone. And on the mount overlooking Rephidim he held it up and Joshua defeated the enemy. He never used the rod without it winning the day and meeting the need.

Before we leave the case of Moses and the rod there is one rather sad proposition I must add.

Proposition seven: *Wrong usage of the rod of God is tragic.*

You will remember that Moses owned the rod in a different sense after the encounter in chapter four. It was his only as it was God's. He held it by the lesser end and he must always remember that it belonged to him only in the will of God. God was to govern its usage and he could never act as if it was his. We must always keep this in mind.

Again and again in the sight of the people Moses obeyed and used the rod as an instrument of divine power. It is so easy to become presumptuous even with spiritual things.

And one day Moses became peeved with his congregation. The situation is described in Psalm 106:32-33, "They angered him also at the waters of strife, so that it went ill with Moses for their sakes: because they PROVOKED HIS SPIRIT so that he spake unadvisedly with his lips."

The historical event is recorded in Numbers 20. They had run out of water again and were chiding Moses as they had before. God told Moses to take the rod and speak to the rock in order to get water. Moses had lost patience. Their complaining had plainly provoked him. He says: "Hear now, ye rebels; must we fetch you water out of this rock?" (Num. 20:10).

Moses then struck the rock, not once but twice. This is a liberty that no man who stands in God's power can afford to take. Such a seemingly slight offense it was . . . but it shortened the life of Moses. He was denied the privilege of going into the land toward which he had looked so long. I once made the statement that he never got to enter the land—until my son, then about twelve years of age, reminded me that Moses did come to the land when he and Elijah visited with Jesus on the mount of transfiguration! God made it clear that the reason for the punishment was his disobedience. "And the Lord spake unto Moses and Aaron, Because ye believed me not, to sanctify me in the eyes of the children of Israel, therefore ye shall not bring this congregation into the land which I have given them" (Num. 20:12) Then again in Deuteronomy 32:48-52 we read: "And the Lord spake unto Moses the selfsame day, saying, Get thee up . . . unto mount Nebo . . . and behold the land which I give unto the children of Israel for a possession: and die in the mount

. . . because ye trespassed against me among the children of Israel at the waters of Meribah-Kadesh, in the wilderness of Zin; because ye sanctified me not in the midst of the children of Israel. Yet thou shalt see the land before thee; but thou shalt not go hither unto the land which I give the children of Israel."

Moses' offense: HE DISOBEYED GOD IN THE USE OF THE ROD. He forgot for the moment that it was not his rod to do with as he desired. Wrong usage of the gifts of God are destructive. WHAT IS THAT IN YOUR HAND?

In closing this chapter let me put this question to you. What is that in your hand? Is it a plan, a man, a position, a gift, a talent? Is it a church, a situation, a sum of money? Is it a wife, children, parents, brothers or sisters? You may deem it good or bad . . . but CAST IT DOWN BEFORE THE LORD! Remember that it has a snake in the relationship before it is thrown down before the Lord.

Are you hesitating? Resorting to reason? It doesn't make sense, does it? Why do you hesitate to put it down before the Lord? You had not realized it was as precious to you as it seems now? You may lose it but it will be the prerogative of your heavenly Father to cleanse it of self and give it back to you. I discovered that I never really possessed my family until I possessed them *in the Lord.*

Once everything in your life is before the Lord you can give yourself to his control. He in you can control your life, govern your behavior, and direct your destiny according to his wisdom. One by one take every possession which is yours and transfer the ownership to the Lord. Present yourself to him in the totality of your being.

As it was with Moses so it will be with you. "THOU SHALT TAKE THIS ROD WHEREWITH THOU SHALT DO SIGNS!"

CONTINUE ON! REMEMBER THE ROD OF GOD

11
Walking on the Water

Following the Lord Jesus is much akin to the experience of walking on the water. You can depend on none of the former things to support you. You are, as it were, out and out on Jesus. If he does not come through, you are sunk. By walking on the water a little, you learn a lot about what happens after the Spirit comes.

JRT

"Jesus spake unto them, saying, Be of good cheer; It is I; be not afraid. And Peter answered him and said, Lord if it be thou, bid me come unto thee on the water. And he [Jesus] said, Come. And when Peter was come down out of the ship, *he walked on the water,* to go to Jesus" (Matt. 14:27-29).

When the Spirit comes in power, we are called to "walk on water." We are invited to an overcoming life in which we have the authority to walk on the waves of our turbulent surroundings and head straight for Jesus.

This chapter is not a frivolous invitation to head for the pond nearest you and make an attempt to skip out across the surface. It is an invitation for you to get out of the boat of ordinariness and onto the circumstances where trust in God is normal. We shall learn much by this exciting episode of a mortal man walking on water.

Meet Peter. Here was a man who seemed to have an aversion for the average, a built-in repulsion for ordinariness. He is the crown prince of the unexpected, the unique, the sensational. He was one of those all-too-rare folks who could not let well enough alone. If folks should have patron saints, Peter should be the patron saint of the reckless. He seemed to be "an accident waiting for the right time and place to happen" . . . and seldom happened at either the right time or the right place.

But for all his bumblings, fumblings, mistakes, and jumping-the-gun errors he becomes an unavoidable challenge to all of us to jump out of the boat of the commonplace and out onto the sea of adventure in following Christ.

What is it to walk on water? I am asking in the spiritual realm. There is surely a spiritual counterpart of physical water-walking. It is that moment of truth when we decide to climb out on God and put our weight so much on his providence that if he does not *come* through we *are* through! It is the *refusal* of the status quo, the *receiving* of Jesus' orders, and the *revival* of faith. It is the identification of one's self with Jesus in his overcoming and the sharing of his dominion. It is the Christocentric life, the Spirit-filled life, the God-anointed life. It is the walk of faith . . . a life of glorious uncertainties from the human view in order to view the certainties from the divine vantage point!

This chapter is an invitation, a challenge to leave your boat of security and sameness, whatever it might be, and get out on Jesus! This is where the action is!

Some Things You Should Know About Walking on Water

1. *The challenge to walk on water may confront us in darkness and trouble.* The disciples were in darkness and in trouble that night. They were at the mercy of the turbulent sea. It was between three and six o'clock in the morning. Don't be surprised if right in the middle of trouble and darkness there is the mandate to walk on water.

2. *God allows such a confrontation always to enlarge, never to endanger.* Be sure that the trouble through which you are passing and the darkness which hangs over you are there to help and not to hurt.

3. *You should set identities straight before you try to walk on water.* Though Jesus had just said: "Be of good cheer; it is I, be not afraid" Peter wanted to be double sure. He said: "Lord, if it

be thou, bid me come to thee on the water." Once the issue of identity was settled Peter was ready for business. If we could simply receive a word from the Lord and launch out on him, what a day would come to the kingdom of God! Dare we say this today? "Lord, if that is you out there, just give me the word and I will come to you on the circumstances, right in the face of every wind that blows." We are always wanting Jesus to come to us. He wants us to come to him!

4. *Walking on the water is an opportunity for a lasting victory.* While we are busy talking about what all God has done for us, the world is waiting for word of all that God did for himself through us! Everybody knew that it was not Peter alone who walked on the water. A normal, ordinary, mortal man just doesn't do a thing like that! The world is apt to pay more attention to things it cannot explain. This episode could not be explained except in terms of God!

There are two things which called Peter to walk on water: *One, he saw Jesus conquering, and, two, he heard Jesus calling.* Jesus' personal triumph over the waves and the wind and Jesus' personal call to Peter were invitations enough. "It is I, COME!" Thus, Jesus' *walk* and Jesus' *word* were enough to get Peter out on the water.

Today there is call abroad in the land for faith. The wave-compelling, wind-conquering Savior calls us to share his victory in this storm-tossed age. There are ruinous tempests uncalmed and fearful saints unnerved. The world is waiting for a standard-bearer . . . THIS IS A DAY FOR WALKING ON WATER.

We will look at four areas of truth in the discussion which follows: *Reasons, requisites, rules,* and *rewards* for walking on water.

Reasons for Walking on Water

What are the reasons behind the challenge to get out of the boat of sameness and into a new dimension of life. Basically there are two very good reasons.

The first is dissatisfaction with boat-life. We have identified boat-life with mediocrity, ordinariness, or status quo. Let us look at such a life for a few moments. Here are some of its characteristics.

Boat life is *dull.* It may be safe but it is sour. There may be a minimum of trouble but there is also a minimum of triumph. One of the great problems of this age is boredom. Monotony is misery.

Most folks who have insisted on living the same, tame, lame life of noncommitment are bored to death!

Boat life is *guilt-ridden*. We are made for pressure. We are constructed for a challenge. We are built for battle. The human body does not grow without antagonism. When we allow ourselves to settle into patterns of living that are unchallenging, we are filled with guilt. There is written within the framework of the human spirit certain laws of responsibility which when denied light up like a "tilt" sign on a pinball machine. Our culture may be getting by easy, but the price for it is a guilt-ridden generation.

Boat life is a life of virtual *helplessness*. If you stay in the boat you are generally at the mercy of the waves. Whichever way the wind is blowing is the way that the boat will go. Peter and the disciples were out on the sea being tossed about without any control on their circumstances. If the constituents of the churches today insist in staying in the boat of tradition and compromise, we will find ourselves at the mercy of trends in our society, whether they be economic trends, political trends, or social trends. Folks in the boat are at the mercy of the waves.

Boat life is *unproductive*. The unchallenged life is an unproductive life. God has made us to respond at best to constant pressure. We will not believe if we do not have to. And after a while we will become so accustomed to boat life that we will be helpless in the storms of life.

I have no trouble believing that Peter was tired of the life that never launched out on the reality of Jesus. He could not brook with that sort of company.

The second reason for walking on water is the desire to get out to Jesus. There is never any other proper motive than this. He is where the action is. And if we are not out there where he is, we will never trust like we should. We are ever sinking back down to the level of our environment. Are you out where Jesus is? Would you be willing as did Peter to say to Jesus now, "Lord, if it be you, bid me come to you!" You will respond in the midst of the storms of life in one manner or another. Playing it safe will cause the sea to master you or going for Jesus will cause you to master the sea.

Fix these reasons in your mind . . . dissatisfaction with boat life and a desire to get out to Jesus.

Requisites for Walking on Water

First, the desire to get to Jesus must be greater than the fear of the unknown. The enemy uses fear to back us away from God's best. A lady came to me after a service recently and said: "I have this problem. I would love to give my whole life to God and be filled with the Spirit but I am afraid." I simply said to her, "My dear, until your desire factor rises over your fear factor God can do you little good." If you are to walk on the water of your circumstances to Jesus, your desires must rise above your fears.

Second, there must be the willingness to fail. The passion to succeed is a mark of these days. Threatened failure has caused many a saint to be hesitant to really give all to Jesus. Any time a man steps out of the boat there is the possibility of failure. The man who fears to fail may falter. Not until Peter was willing to be a complete failure was he able to step out of the boat. He must have been willing to be the laughing stock of his group of friends. Look at it this way, you are a failure already. I had rather be a failure heading for Jesus than a failure who never tried back in the boat!

Third, there must be a commitment to Jesus. Peter, when he sought to confirm the identity of Jesus, had already made a commitment. "If it be you . . . bid me come." He was really saying, "Lord, I am coming to you *if it is you.*" Peter had already made up his mind what he would do and made his commitment. This is the disposition which the God-pleasing saint must keep. Whenever there is a storm, it may be another invitation to get out of the boat and fellowship with Jesus out among the waves.

Fourth, there must be a commitment from Jesus. This is left out of most preaching on commitment today. It is of vital importance for you and me to consider our decision to make a commitment to Jesus. It is of even more vital importance that our commitment be of such quality that Jesus makes his commitment to us. Not until our faith is such that God can have faith in our faith is there victory. Peter made such a commitment that Jesus made his commitment to Peter's commitment. He gave Peter one word, "Come!" That was all that was needed. For that one word was at the same time a *command* and a *promise.* God never calls us to do something that he does not empower us to do. Jesus, when he said to Peter, "Come!" was also saying, "You are able!" Whom God *enlists,* he *enlightens.* Whom he *enlightens,* he *empowers.* Have you gotten your commitment from Jesus?

Fifth, the first step must be taken. The longest trip begins with a step. A walk is but a series of steps and there always has to be a first one. That first step out of the boat and onto the water may be the most difficult, but it has to be. For Peter it was simply to put one foot over the side of the boat and get at it! For you, it may be a step toward getting right with a friend, giving up a position, or yielding to God's special all. And God will see to it that you will never be able to see your way clear. Otherwise, faith would be without premium. Don't be concerned about step number five or five thousand. Just take the first and the rest will come easier.

Are you considering the cost of this kind of living? Do you consider the price too high to pay for total commitment to God's way of life? Hundreds of thousands of people today are seeing the folly of giving priority to anything that is not associated with eternity. What else is there worthwhile under the sun? We are not apt to be changed from glory into glory if we insist on staying in the boat of sameness. Many Christians I know are like a soap opera . . . hung up on one scene. You can keep up with most soap operas by watching once a month. You can always predict the next episode. Likewise the unchallenged Christian is predictable and tame.

Do you have what it takes to walk on the water? If your desire to be with Jesus in maximum living greater than your fear? Are you willing to fail? Have you made such a commitment to Jesus that he has made his commitment to you? Are you ready to take the first step? Then let us go on!

Rules for Walking on Water

Out on the water the waves are high. There are threats and uncertainties. Nowhere in his salvation promises did Jesus promise an easy time to his followers. There is something you and I should know when we step out on faith to follow Jesus . . . normal rules do not apply out here. Boat rules will not work out on the water. You can throw your how-to-do-it books away. If you will get out on God, he will run you out of "flesh" methods and bring you to the point that if God does not come through you are finished! We must come to the place where we had rather sink than spend the rest of our lives in the boat!

We have already seen that when the Spirit of God moves in mighty power there are perils. In the rules we will observe there are three "don'ts" and one "do."

Don't look at the waves. "But when he saw the wind boisterous, he was afraid" (Matt. 14:30). Don't be distracted by your difficulties. Remember that Jesus said, "In the world ye shall have tribulation: but be of good cheer; I have overcome the world" (John 16:33). When you get out on the waves walking toward Jesus, don't let the size of those waves bother you. Remember that when King Jehoshaphat took one look at the problems, he fastened his eyes on the Lord and said, in effect, "Lord, we have so many problems that we don't know what to do . . . BUT OUR EYES ARE ON YOU!" When Peter saw what the wind was doing, he took his eyes off what Jesus was doing.

Don't listen to the boat. You can never depend on man to give you the right answer. The simple reason is that men cannot agree. When you step out of the boat, you will get free unsolicited advice from a myriad of folks who have never walked on the water themselves. They are ready, however, to give you proper instructions on how to stay at it.

In the earlier days of my spiritual pilgrimage, I was affected much more by what people said and thought than I am now. I discovered, however, the senselessness of listening to others with a view of receiving final truth. As I began some serious direction changes in my own life a few years ago, I received all sorts of advice. Of course, I couldn't take it all because if I had I would have been doing "opposites" most all the time. I felt like the lady who went to the old-fashioned mourners' bench and well-intentionēd friends were trying to help her. One was saying: "Let go! Let go!" The other was saying in the other ear: "Hang on! Hang on!" One was saying "Fight it out!" The other was saying, "Give up!" Jeremiah's advice was good: "Cease ye from man whose breath is in his nostrils, for whereof shall he be accounted of." It is simply not wise to put terminal trust in what "they" are saying whoever "they" are!

Another good rule is . . . don't look at your feet. In other words, don't become preoccupied with your own "spirituality." We have already encountered the peril of spiritual pride. Many people have stepped out on the adventure of following Jesus only to discover too soon that they were becoming spiritual. "Look at myself! I wonder how I'm doing it!" Begin to look at your own feet to seek to discover how it is that you are walking on water and you too will begin to sink.

Enough for the "don'ts" . . . here is one marvelous "do." *Keep your eyes stayed on Jesus.* The *wind-worrier* will not be a *Savior-seeker.* Either the Savior will rule out the wind or the wind will rule out the Savior. You cannot look at the waves and at Jesus at the same time.

> Turn your eyes upon Jesus,
> Look full in His wonderful face,
> And the things of earth
> Will grow strangely dim,
> In the light of His glory and grace!

Rewards for Walking on Water

I can think of seven rewards right away for walking on water. There are many others, but these will do for now.

One, you get to leave the boat. You experience deliverance from calculated living. You experience the discovery of your own individuality instead of hiding in the crowd.

Two, you get to fail! Now that is a strange reward isn't it? But Peter, out on the water, experienced failure. And that failure was a cue to Jesus to enter with salvation. He has never been saved who did not recognize his own failure in life. The whole scheme of salvation is constructed on the failure of humanity. Had not Peter failed, he would have never needed to cry, "Lord, save me!" The best things happen to us when we acknowledge our failure and move into his success. The greatest successes have been driven to succeed by failure. It is good to remember that every miracle began with a problem or failure.

Three, you get to be rescued. I am always having to get rescued. Out on the water we live next to our failure so as to live next to his success. We live close to our weakness so as to live next to his strength. If I do not stay aware of the fact that I *need* him every hour, I lose sight of the fact that I *have* him every hour. Salvation is more than just an event because of which we go to heaven when we die. It is a living relationship and a lasting process. I have been saved . . . that is an *appointed event*. I am being saved . . . that is *present experience*. I will be saved . . . that is *positive eventuality*. Only those who know what it feels like to be sinking know what it feels like to be rescued!

Four, you get to go to Jesus. That was the goal of Peter. "He walked on the water, to go to Jesus" (Matt. 14:29). You really don't mind where you are if you can sense that you are with Jesus, even if you are in trouble up to your ears. Those early disciples found their joy in going with Jesus. Are you with him right now? Get on faith, believing him and he will not be ashamed to accompany you anywhere he leads you to go.

Five, you get to walk with Jesus. Getting to Jesus is only part of the experience. Going on with him in a continuous walk is glorious. The walk may sometimes be punctuated by periods of failure but please remember that after Peter's experience of sinking he continued his walk with Jesus once he was rescued. It took Jesus no time to lift Peter up and restore him to walk with him. Then they walked to the boat together.

Six, you get where you are going. In John's narrative of this episode he says, "And immediately the ship was at the land whither they went" (John 6:21). Many folks accuse a person of losing direction when he follows Jesus. In Peter's case every step he took with Jesus was a step nearer where he was going in the first place. While everyone was watching Peter and Jesus, the providence of God was at work to deposit them at their intended destination. After all, they were on the sea at his orders and he knew their appointed destination. Have you gotten where you are going?

Seven, you get to worship Jesus. Matthew's record says, "And when they were come into the ship, the wind ceased. Then they that were in the ship came and worshipped him, saying, Of a truth thou art the Son of God" (Matt. 14:32-33). It is marvelous to worship Jesus. It is much more thrilling to worship him after you have been out on the water walking with him through the storm. This is the reason that the folks who have the most inward peace are those who have known the greatest storms. They have discovered a Savior who can walk with them in the storm, carry them through it, and arrive with them safely at the appointed and intended port. How long has it been since you joyously exclaimed, "Of a truth, you are the Son of God"? It was probably the last time that you found yourself in a set of circumstances which brought Jesus to you walking on the water to prove himself strong to save.

Do you not hear the Lord beckoning us all to a higher life? "It is I . . . be not afraid . . . come!"

The reasons for walking on water are relevant.

The requisites for walking on water are real.

The rules for walking on water are rigid.

The rewards for walking on water are rich.

12
A Faith for the Fiery Furnace

There is apparently a law operating in the spiritual realm that guarantees that when the Spirit of God moves to initiate and implement the plans of God . . . the enemy will come to oppose it. This opposition may be subtle and gradual or fierce and violent. However it is, you can be sure that if you set your face to follow the Spirit you will need a faith for the fiery furnace.

JRT

"Without faith it is impossible to please him: for he that cometh to God must believe that he is, and that he is a rewarder of them that diligently seek him" (Heb. 11:6).

Don't expect a reception in your honor when you decide to begin your walk in the Spirit. The exact opposite is liable to occur. This chapter is for all who have cast their lots with him whatever the cost. It is for all those who have or one day soon will know about fires and furnaces in personal experience. It is true that every believer who really means business with God will know the hard place, the trial, the testing time. For Shadrach, Meshach, and Abednego it was a literal furnace and literal fire, but they stand in a long line of believers who have suffered for their faith only to reveal to the world a clear view of Jesus, the Christ. Honorable mention is given to these men in Hebrews 11. It simply says, "quenched the violence of fire."

There is no more thrilling story in literature than the story of the three Hebrews and their experience with the fiery furnace. If saints in tight places needed patron saints, Shadrach, Meshach, and

Abednego would have my vote as prime prospects. Here were three men, who along with Daniel, were experiencing continuous revival. Though they were in a foreign land they were not controlled by its rules. They listened to another's voice and ate of the fare of heaven. Their persistence under pressure should at once be a challenge and a comfort to us all.

Let's rehearse the historical setting for this marvelous story. In the fading years of the sixth century b.c., Nebuchadnezzar, the powerful king of Babylon, besieged Jerusalem, confiscated many of the vessels from the house of God, and carried the choicest young people into Babylon. The King gave orders that Ashpenaz, the master of the eunuchs, "should bring certain of the children of Israel, and of the king's seed, and of the princes; children in whom was no blemish, but well favoured, and skilful in all wisdom, and cunning in knowledge, and understanding science, and such as had ability in them to stand in the king's palace" (Dan. 1:3-4).

Four of these children of Israel immediately distinguished themselves in the palace of the king for their faithfulness to the God of Israel. They refused the finery and the fare of the king's table. They purposed in their hearts that they would not defile themselves with the portion of the king's meat.

Thus Shadrach, Meshach, Abednego, and Daniel had come to the kingdom for such a time as this. The record is that "God gave them knowledge and skill in all learning and wisdom" (Dan. 1:17).

After three years, these choice young people were to be presented to the king, having mastered the arts and sciences and the Chaldean language. As the king of Babylon communed with them, he found none like these four who had remained faithful to God. "And in all matters of wisdom and understanding, that the king enquired of them, he found them ten times better than all the magicians and astrologers that were in his realm" (Dan. 1:20).

Well, it looked like revival was inevitable in the king's palace with these four faithful men in positions of influence. To enhance the situation, Nebuchadnezzar dreamed a dream which he promptly forgot and yet demanded an interpretation of it. Daniel was the only one in the kingdom who could interpret the unknown dream. He revealed his source of information when he said: "But there is a God in heaven that revealeth secrets. . . . But as for me this secret is not revealed to me for any wisdom that I have any more than any living" (Dan. 2:28,30). When Daniel was finished with the interpretation, the king of Babylon fell upon his face and worshiped Daniel and commanded an offering to be made unto him. The king exclaimed: "Of a truth it is, that your God is a God of gods, and a Lord of kings, and a revealer of secrets" (Dan. 2:47). It was then that Daniel was promoted to greatness in the kingdom and was appointed ruler over the whole province of Babylon and chief of the governors over all the wise men of Babylon. Daniel's one request was that his three friends, Shadrach, Meshach, and Abednego, be placed in charge of the affairs of the province of Babylon. This request was promptly carried out.

Then a strange thing happened. The king constructed a gigantic image of gold, placed it on the plain of Dura, and demanded that when certain music was played all the people should fall down and worship the image. Violation of this rule would be penalized by instant death in the fiery furnace.

Guess who wouldn't bow! The three high-up cabinet officials, Shadrach, Meshach, and Abednego, refused to worship any other but the God of Israel. They were immediately accused and hauled in before the king. The king was willing to give them another chance but threatened them that if they did not bow and worship the image they should be cast the same hour in the fiery furnace. He asked, "Who is that God that shall deliver you out of my hands?" (Dan. 3:15). The response of the three Hebrew children is worthy of note: "O Nebuchadnezzar, we are not careful to answer thee in this matter. If it be so, our God whom we serve is able to deliver us from the burning fiery furnace, and he will deliver us out of thine hand, O king. BUT IF NOT, be it known unto thee, O king, that we will not serve thy gods, nor worship the golden image which thou hast set up" (Dan. 3:16-18). Now there wasn't anything indefinite about that stand was there?

King Nebuchadnezzar flew into an absolute rage, commanded the fiery furnace to be heated seven times hotter than usual, and ordered his mighty men to bind Meshach, Shadrach, and Abednego and cast them into the furnace. It was done and the fire was so hot that the men who cast them into the furnace were burned to death at the furnace entrance.

We shall leave these three for a few moments to talk of similar experiences in the lives of all God's children. It may not be a fiery furnace but there will be some means that the enemy will contrive to seek to destroy us. But God will use these experiences to serve our better ends. To Jehoshaphat it was an invading army. To John it was Patmos Isle and banishment. To Paul it was prison and suffering. Whatever the shape of the crucible, God loves us so much that he is willing to put us in tight places, so he can reveal himself mighty to save. I want to make four observations as we come to view the prospects of *a faith for the fiery furnace.*

Observation one: Furnace experiences are bound to come. Set your determination to follow the Lord and the enemy will see to it that there are plots and opposition against you. Trouble has flanked the path of believers and followers of God since the beginning. God has not promised that we will be spared trouble but that he will be with us in it. The furnace for you may be a set of puzzling circumstances, a shocking event, a difficult adjustment, or one of a thousand other things . . . but it is bound to come.

Observation two: Trouble does not have to be tragic though this is the typical human evaluation of it. It matters greatly how we react in times of trouble. Trouble can be spelled two ways. Most folks spell it t-r-a-g-e-d-y. Some have found the secret of the Lord and have learned to spell it t-r-i-u-m-p-h! In the economy of God trouble, antagonism, and pressures are useful in shaping us into his image. We will see that when the episode is over, God, his people, and his cause are all bettered. How do you spell trouble? How you spell it will make all the difference in the world how it comes out.

Observation three: Loyalty in the midst of trouble brings results worth reading about. Have you read the eleventh chapter of Hebrews lately? Have you noticed how many of those saints had a faith that was born and nurtured in the furnace of trial and trouble. Had it not been for trouble in their lives as a platform for the building of their faith, we may never have read about them. Of what worth would the testimonies of these men have been had they capitulated to the demands of the king and worshiped the image? They were loyal to their God and their God vindicated their faith. Our conduct under pressure may well be our most significant ministry. Our deportment in the furnace may tell the world more about our God than all the witnessing we could ever do. The whole plot of the convincing eleventh chapter of Hebrews is that of *faithfulness in the fire.* The whole chapter is God's great commercial amplifying the quality of the life that wins. It will be so in your life and mine that when we are loyal in times of trouble God will proudly let the story out to his glory.

Observation four: Need is necessary. I have said it in so many words but I believe that it needs to be specifically spelled out. The equation is clear in Paul's mysterious "thorn in the flesh" confrontation . . . God's strength was made perfect in his weakness. Had there been no weakness, there would have been no strength. Need is necessary for supply. Paul affirmed, "My God shall *supply* all your *need* according to his riches in glory by Christ Jesus" (Phil. 4:19). If there is no need, there is no supply. If there is no battle there is no victory.

I spent the last days of 1973 in the Swiss mountains in the French Highland section of Switzerland. I was all alone the last few minutes of the very last day of the year. As the fading seconds of 1973 ticked away, I was recounting the blessings of God upon my life during the year. I could not conceive that God could ever do anymore in the next year than he had done in the one just past. It was joy unspeakable and full of glory. The question that pierced my consciousness was, How can I know more of God's power and provision the coming seasons than in the last ones? The word that shot back into my awareness was "need." I was puzzled for a moment. Why is the key word "need"? I asked myself. Then the verse came to me, "My God shall supply *all your need.*" That is it . . . the secret. If you would have more of *God's supply,* then you must experience more of *human need.* The greater the need the greater the supply. Praise the Lord. So I quietly asked God to give me greater needs! He has graciously answered that prayer and his supply has matched the needs as he promised!

Now let's look at this faith forged in the fiery furnace. I want us to look at *the requisites of such a faith, the revelations of such a faith,* and finally at *the results of such a faith.*

The Requisites of Such a Faith

The strength of faith is never any greater than the object of its trust. Total faith in a powerless entity is futile. The whole platform of faith is the power and providence of God. This is the first requisite . . . *the existence of and belief in the overruling and undergirding providence of God.* Now if you miss this you will miss the whole matter. God is engineering your whole set of circumstances. He has not left you to the cruel clutches of fate! God not only engineers your circumstances and mine . . . HE *IS* OUR CIRCUMSTANCES! Norman Grubb says, "Joseph learned the first lesson of obedience. God was his circumstance, God his environment: it is not in self to order our outward way aright; our very enemies are carrying out God's plan for us."

God is still in charge. His dominion stands firm. He has not lost out in his world. His plans have not been abandoned. They are still moving along on schedule.

Because God was omniscient, he knew about the company that manufactured the furnace, its patent number and copyright information. Being *omnipresent* he was there to oversee the construction and installment of it. He was there through the whole episode. Being *omnipotent* he was greater than the sum total of all the kings of earth. He had placed Nebuchadnezzar on the throne of Babylon and presided over the affairs which found his own favored children in the flames of that furnace. They could say: "God knows we are here and is in it with us! Hallelujah!"

The second requisite to this kind of faith is *consistency in common responsibilities.* You see these three men had an unblemished record of faithfulness in little things. If our trust is rigid in the *minute* things, God will bring it to face *major* things. Everybody wants to stand in the days of faith's victory but few are willing to stand in the days of faith's testing. Most of us want the diploma but are not willing to go through what it takes to prepare the homework. Shadrach, Meshach, and Abednego were men who had tried and proved God in the small things of life and thus when the big trouble came they were able to trust him. The faith that will stand in the fiery furnace is a faith which has distinguished itself by consistency in life's common commitments.

The third requisite for this faith is *an irrevocable commitment to the trustworthiness of God.* I want you to get this. The next paragraph is probably the most vital word in this whole story. We have discussed it briefly in the chapter entitled "When God Doesn't Come Through." The three Hebrew children did not stutter or hesitate when they made known their stand to the king. The whole basis of their commitment was, "OUR GOD IS ABLE!" If that is settled in our minds, the commitment is irrevocable. As long as that is our heartfelt affirmation, faith has a firm basis. OUR GOD IS ABLE! This is the issue.

Do you believe that God is able? Your response is probably like mine . . . I don't have problems with God's ability but with God's willingness to act. And to that I reply that our commitment to him must be so unconditional that if he doesn't act we will still trust him. Job's commitment was such that he was able to say, "Though he slay me, yet will I trust him." And here Shadrach, Meshach, and Abednego are saying in effect: "O king, we know that God is able. That is a settled fact. Whether he delivers us from the furnace and from your hands or not does not change our conviction that he is able. If he does not deliver us . . . we will still refuse to serve your gods or bow down to worship your image." If our commitment is to be irrevocable we must settle the possibilities of the "but-if-nots." If you claim to have lost faith because of a situation in which God did not come through in the manner you expected, then this is proof that your faith was more in God's acts than in God himself. When your faith is in God himself there will be no disappointments for that faith.

The glory of the commitment of the three Hebrew children was that it was not conditioned on any circumstances. God was not on trial in this situation. His reputation was established. GOD IS ABLE!

Thus we have three planks in the platform of a faith for the fiery furnace: One, *the existence of and belief in the overruling and undergirding providence of God;* two, *a consistency in common responsibilities;* and three, *an irrevocable commitment to the trustworthiness of God.*

The Revelations of Such a Faith

There is first, *the revelation of deliverance.* And what a deliverance it was! These three faithful were thrust into the furnace heated seven times hotter than normal. It was so hot that the mighty men who cast them in were killed instantly. The biblical record is: "And these three men, Shadrach, Meshach, and Abednego, fell down bound into the midst of the burning fiery furnace" (Dan. 3:23). God's methods of deliverance are often strange. Why could God not have kept them from the furnace? He could have! But his glorious providence demonstrated his ability to master the flames within the furnace. Why should God do the easier thing when the accomplishing of the impossible would reveal his greater glory? The stories of God's deliverances are unutterably thrilling. He delivered his children from the Egyptians at the Red Sea, delivered them daily from starvation and death, and continued to nurture and care for them. He surrounded his prophets with armies of angels. He fought for his people and never lost! But as glorious as is his deliverance, it is not the most important thing. There is another revelation brought about by great faith.

It is *the revelation of the DELIVERER.* We are prone to get preoccupied with the deliverance to the neglect of our deliverer. Their deliverance *from* the furnace was not nearly so significant as their deliverance *in* the furnace. This is a vital point. Why should God deliver you from a situation before that situation has had its intended ministry in you? He has brought you into this circumstance to reveal to you and through you not only God's power to deliver, but to reveal through you God's PERSON, THE DELIVERER . . . none other than the Lord Jesus Christ.

Regarding this most important point, listen to the king's report in astonishment, "Did not we cast three men bound into the fire? . . . Lo, I see four men loose, walking in the midst of the fire and they have no hurt; and the form of the fourth is like the Son of God" (Dan. 3:24-25). I want you to get the significance of this mystery:

THREE MEN BOUND, FALLING . . . (Daniel 3:23)
FOUR MEN LOOSE, WALKING . . . (Daniel 3:25)

Three men went through the door into the furnace. They were bound and had to fall down. But as they fell they trusted God. Faith reveals the *deliverer.* I believe that this is one of those rare visible preincarnate visits of the Lord Jesus to this earth. I can imagine that Jesus speaks to the Father as the plot thickens, "Father, let me go and stand with our friends in the midst of the fire!" The Father says, "Now, Son, stand with them!" And there he was! The *form of the fourth* appeared in the midst of the fire. The king knew nothing of theology but he caught glimpse enough of the fourth man to know that he was more than a man!

And alas, notice that they are loose, not bound. The fire has served only to burn away the bonds! And now they walk with Jesus.

The Results of Such a Faith

A faith for the fiery furnace is a faith that yields joyous results. Let us view them briefly:

First, it confirms the Son. All the claims of Jesus are confirmed in the crucible of faith. His promise is that he will never leave us or forsake us. The king, though a heathen, bore testimony that there was someone present in the furnace who was like a god. Faith under trial always confirms Jesus.

Second, it consumes the bonds and the binders. The flames of trial serve to break our fetters and consume the ones who bound us. In this case the ones who bound the three Hebrew children were burned to death. The fire will affect only that which binds us. You will notice that in the severe testings of faith those things that serve to limit will be burned away in the fire of the furnace. Praise God for the furnace!

Third, it clears the saints and commissions them to higher offices. "Then Shadrach, Meshach, and Abednego, came forth out of the midst of the fire" (Dan. 3:26). They came out without a blister. Listen to the detailed description of their condition: "saw these men upon whose bodies the fire had no power, nor was a hair of their head singed, neither were their coats changed, nor the smell of fire had passed on them" (Dan. 3:27). There was not even the smell of smoke on them! Praise the Lord! They were then promoted in the province of Babylon!

Fourth, it convinces the world of the greatness of God. The princes, the governors, the captains, and the king's counselors were all gathered to behold the phenomenon. It was then that old King Nebuchadnezzar has himself a shouting spell! Listen to his doxology, spontaneously delivered:

BLESSED BE THE GOD OF SHADRACH, MESHACH, AND ABEDNEGO, WHO HATH SENT HIS ANGEL, AND DELIVERED HIS SERVANTS THAT TRUSTED IN HIM, AND HAVE CHANGED THE

KING'S WORD, AND YIELDED THEIR BODIES, THAT THEY MIGHT NOT SERVE NOR WORSHIP ANY GOD, EXCEPT THEIR OWN GOD. Therefore I make a decree, that every people, nation, and language, which speak anything amiss against the God of Shadrach, Meshach, and Abednego, shall be cut in pieces, and their houses shall be made a dunghill; BECAUSE THERE IS NO OTHER GOD THAT CAN DELIVER AFTER THIS SORT! (Dan. 3:28-29).

The king continues his adulation in the next chapter:

"Peace be multiplied unto you. I thought it good to shew the signs and wonders that the high God hath wrought toward me. How great are his signs! And how mighty are his wonders! His kingdom is an everlasting kingdom, and his dominion is from generation to generation!" (Dan. 4:1-3).

Dear saint, God is able! Establish that as a prime truth and whatever happens you won't *bow, budge, or burn!* That is the story of the Hebrew children. They wouldn't bow, they wouldn't budge, and they didn't burn! I trust that your faith is a faith that will stand the fiery furnace.

13
The Church's Greatest Ministry

The last three chapters of this volume deal with the matter of direction. After the Spirit comes . . . what then? Where then? Direction is all-important.

Three directions best define the priorities of the believer and the church in following the Spirit:

UPWARD . . . *Spotlights the church's greatest ministry . . . prayer.*

INWARD . . . *Emphasizes the ministry of love within the body.*

OUTWARD . . . *Places the premium on total evangelism.*

JRT

"And he said unto them, It is written, My house shall be called the house of prayer; but ye have made it a den of thieves." (Matt. 21:13).

"What the church needs today is not more machinery or better, not new organizations or more and novel methods, but men whom the Holy Ghost can use . . . men of prayer, men mighty in prayer" (Edward M. Bounds).[1]

The Price of Prayerlessness

Samuel recognized prayerlessness to be a sin when he said in 1 Samuel 12:23: "Moreover as for me, God forbid that I should sin against the Lord in ceasing to pray for you."

Prayerlessness costs in three directions. It costs others; it costs God; and it costs us.

First, there is the price of rebellion. If you and I are not praying, we are sinning because prayerlessness is a sin. It is a command to pray. To violate a command of God is to sin. God cannot pour out his blessings upon a rebellious heart. God not only invites us to pray, he commands us to pray. He ordered Jeremiah to "Call unto me, and I will answer thee, and show thee great and mighty things, which thou knowest not" (Jer. 33:3). God gave the command through Isaiah, "Seek ye the Lord while he may be found, call ye upon him while he is near" (Isa. 55:6). Jesus gave clear command in the Sermon on the Mount to "Ask, and it shall be given you; seek, and ye shall find; knock, and it shall be opened unto you: For everyone that asketh receiveth; and he that seeketh findeth; and to him that knocketh it shall be opened" (Matt. 7:7-8).

Jesus' life was a commandment and a challenge to pray. Such was his prayer life that his disciples asked him on one occasion, "Lord teach us to pray!" Jesus said that men ought always to pray and not to faint. Paul spoke to Timothy about the Christian's responsibilities to others: "I exhort therefore, that, first of all, supplications, prayers, and intercessions, and giving of thanks, be made for all men. I will therefore that men pray every where, lifting up holy hands, without wrath and doubting" (1 Tim. 2:1,8).

Prayerlessness is a refusal of the promises of God, rebellion against the very teachings of Jesus, and a clear violation of the spirit of Scripture.

Second, there is the price of deficiency. James simply says, "Ye have not, because ye ask not" (Jas. 4:2). That is about the size of the situation. If we do not have wisdom, it is a sign that we have not asked God for it. He has said, "If any of you lack wisdom, let him ask of God, that giveth to all men liberally, and upbraideth not; and it shall be given him" (Jas. 1:5). If we do not have revival, it is simply because we have not prayed. God has promised: "If my people, which are called by my name, shall humble themselves, and *pray* and seek my face, and turn from their wicked ways; then will I hear from heaven, and will forgive their sin, and will heal their lands" (2 Chron. 7:14).

Third, there is the price of powerlessness. There is no more power in the church or in the life than there is in prayer. A prayerless ministry is the undertaker to all God's truth and to God's church. No part of the life or ministry will rise to stay above the level of our praying. To remain prayerless is to draw the line past which no part of our spiritual life will go.

The Primacy of Prayer

It isn't that the church or the average Christian does not believe in prayer. They simply do not believe that it should hold a place of primacy, or at least they do not live like it.

If you were asked what the greatest ministry in the church is, what would be your answer? There are many great ministries within the church. There is the Bible-teaching ministry. No one is moved to impugn the value of this ministry. But it is not the most important. Preaching is vital and cannot be substituted for but neither is it the prime ministry of the church. Benevolence is a vital part of the church's ministry. However, it is not the church's greatest ministry. Outreach and soul-winning are absolute necessities in the ministry of the church. But as important as this is it is not the greatest ministry of the church.

The greatest ministry of the church is prayer. S. D. Gordon said, "The greatest thing that a man can do for God is to pray. It is not the only thing. But it is the chief thing. A correct balancing of the possible powers one may exert puts it first. For if a man is to pray right, he must first be right in his motives and life. And if a man be right, and put the practice of praying in the right place, then his serving and giving and speaking will be fairly fragrant with the presence of God." [2]

When Jesus walked into the Temple, he took time to survey the situation and to make a whip. His was a clear case of premeditated anger. He became rather violent . . . in fact more violent than we have ever known him to be. He physically cast people out of the Temple, overthrew their money tables, and actually drove them out! In explaining his actions he said, "My house shall be called the house of prayer; but ye have made it a den of thieves." That statement didn't bother me much until one day I began to inquire into the real meaning of it. Why did Jesus become so violent? Well, it was because of something that they were doing that they shouldn't have been doing. They were using the house of the Lord for personal gain.

But that was not the prime offense. This is the realization that shocked me! The prime offense was the neglect to do something that they should have done. Jesus affirmed that his house was to be so much a place of prayer that it would be called a house of prayer. My reasoning continued as I asked myself, What would folks think of your church and its main function upon investigation? There certainly was not enough prayer that would have called for them to conclude that it was a church of prayer. They might have said that it was a church of preaching, or teaching, or evangelism, or even friendliness but they would never have included prayer as its main ministry.

Jesus said that they had turned his house into a den of thieves. Who then is guilty of thievery? It is the person who robs the church of its supreme peculiarity . . . prayer. If we make the church less than a house of prayer we too are thieves. The Temple was holy and what went on in it was important. Now, the Bible confirms that we are the temples of God. Paul told the Corinthians, "Know ye not that ye are the temple of God, and that the Spirit of God dwelleth in you?" (1 Cor. 3:16). If I am God's temple, then I too should be known as a house of prayer. Above every other quality and characteristic, I could be distinguished by prayer. If I am not a house of prayer, then I am no less a robber and a thief than the moneychangers in the Temple. The attitude of Jesus toward thieves has not changed. Fearful reasoning, isn't it?

The disciples asked Jesus an interesting and all-important question when they asked, "What shall we do, that we might work the works of God?" His simple response was, "This is the work of God, that ye believe on him whom he hath sent." Prayer is acting and receiving belief. It is the work of God.

Jesus said: "Verily, verily, I say unto you, He that believeth on me, the works that I do shall he do also; and greater works than these shall he do; because I go unto my Father" (John 14:12). We might have a reason to be puzzled about what Jesus meant were it not for the fact that the very next verse says: "And whatsoever ye shall ask in my name, that will I do that the Father may be glorified in the Son" (John 14:13). There is no doubt that the "greater work" is the work of prayer.

The Purpose of Prayer

Prayer looks out upon three directions . . . toward heaven, earth, and hell. Toward the first it is *worship*. Toward the second it is *work*. Toward the third, it is *warfare*. It is the divinely appointed means of getting God to move from heaven into earth to do his will and defeat hell.

Let us look first at prayer as worship. When the disciples asked Jesus to teach them to pray, he gave them the model prayer. He indicated through its structure that a part of the prayer life was adoration. "Hallowed be thy name," is not merely to be an entrance into prayer but an act of worship in itself. There is power in the very act of praise. Praise liberates the atmosphere and moves God into action. Praise releases the human heart to love God and others. Prayer does not open the way to worship as much as it *is* worship.

Let us look next at prayer as work. We feature prayer too much to be something we do before we work. It is the door, we think, into our activity. We open our committee meetings with it. We open our services with it. We say, in effect, "Let's get prayer out of the way so we can get down to business." We look too little on prayer as business and work in itself. Watchman Nee observes, "Let us understand that the church's noblest work, the greatest task she could ever undertake, is to be the outlet for God's will. For the church to be an outlet for God's will is for her to pray. Such prayer is not fragmentary; it is prayer ministry . . . prayer as *work*. As God gives vision and opens people's eyes to see His will, so people rise up to pray." [3]

If the church addresses itself to its main ministry it will require more workmen and more work than any other ministry. Let us cease to look upon prayer as a mere devotional exercise and view it as a work . . . the main work of the church and of the Christian.

Let us look finally at prayer as warfare. Paul exhorted the Ephesians to be strong in the Lord and in the power of his might. He then described the fearful foes which are arrayed against us . . . principalities and power, rulers of the darkness of this world, spiritual wickedness in high places. He then turns to discuss the armor or the believer from head to foot . . . the helmet of salvation, breastplate of righteousness, girdle of truth, shoes of preparation, shield of faith, and sword of the spirit which is the Word of God. After defining the warriors, wardrobe, weapons, and the wiles of the enemy he then describes the warfare . . . PRAYER! In all my study of the last verses of Ephesians, I did not see this truth until recently. Prayer

is not a prelude to the warfare . . . PRAYER IS THE WARFARE!
The very next verse reveals this . . . "Praying always with all prayer"
(Eph. 6:18).

Listen to what S. D. Gordon says of this: "The greatest agency
put into man's hands is prayer. To understand that at all fully one
needs to define prayer. And to define prayer adequately one must
use the language of war. Peace language is not equal to the situation.
The earth is in a state of war. It is being hotly beseiged and so
one must use war talk to grasp the facts with which prayer is
concerned. *Prayer from God's side is communication between Himself
and His allies in the enemy's country.* True prayer moves in a circle.
It begins with the heart of God, sweeps down into a human heart
upon the earth, so intersecting the circle of the earth which is the
battle-field of prayer, and then it goes back again to its starting
point, having accomplished its purpose of the downward swing." [4]

The Program of Prayer

I have already stated that no part of the church's ministry will
rise to stay above its prayer ministry. I have always believed this
but I have not always practiced it. I realized that the first thing
I must do to be consistent was to give prayer its proper place in
my own life. The next thing must inevitably be the revision of the
church program to include prayer as a matter of priority. Let us
view these two areas as facets of the program of prayer.

One: there is the personal practice of prayer. No group of people
has any more prayer power than the separate individuals. There
is no need to attempt a corporate program of prayer in the church
until there is a revival of prayer in the lives of individuals. I have
several suggestions in this realm. First, become absolutely convinced
that prayer is a matter of personal priority. Declare it to yourself
and confess before God that you will, by his power bring your life
into line with prayer's priority. Determine to do anything that it
takes to make you consistent with this fact.

Second, reevaluate everything in your life as to its importance
and allow to drop from your curriculum those things not absolutely
vital. Check time leaks in your daily schedule, such as too much
time spent reading the newspaper or watching television or secular
reading. Examine your schedule with a view of finding more time.

Prayer is work which will require much time.

Third, begin a program of personal prayer. Do not avoid a plan . . . God uses plans. Have a prayer notebook. In the last few years I have used as a prayer help, a notebook put together by Peter Lord of Titusville, Florida. It has proved to be a very helpful tool in prayer. I have two pages in the beginning of my prayer notebook devoted to praise. I have selected key passages from the Psalms to aid me in learning how to praise the Lord. This comes first in my praying. When I find freedom in praising the Lord, there is great liberty in prayer. The psalmist encourages us to "Enter into his gates with thanksgiving, and into his courts with praise" (Ps. 100:4). It is through praise and thanksgiving that we stand in the mid-court of God's glory!

Some of the praise Scripture passages that I rehearse in prayer are as follows:

Psalm 33:1	Rejoice in the Lord, O ye righteous: for praise is comely in the upright.
Psalm 34:1	I will bless the Lord at all times: his praise shall continually be in my mouth.
Psalm 40:3	And he hath put a new song in my mouth, even praise unto our God: Many shall see it, and fear, and shall trust in the Lord.
Psalm 47:6-7	Sing praise to God, sing praises: sing praises unto our King. God is the King of all the earth: sing ye praises with understanding.
Psalm 48:1	Great is the Lord, and greatly to be praised in the city of our God, in the mountain of his holiness.
Psalm 50:14	Offer unto God thanksgiving; and pay thy vows unto the most High.
Psalm 55:22	Cast thy burden upon the Lord, and he will sustain thee: he shall never suffer the righteous to be moved.
Psalm 57:8-9	Awake up, my glory; awake, psaltry and harp: I myself will awake early. I will praise thee, O Lord, among the people. I will sing unto thee among the nations.
Psalm 61:8	So I will sing praise unto thy name for ever, that I may daily perform my vows.

| Psalm 68:19 | Blessed be the Lord who daily loadeth us with benefits. . . . He that is our God is the God of salvation; and unto God the Lord belong the issues from death. |
| Exodus 15:2 | The Lord is my strength and song, and he is become my salvation: he is my God, and I will prepare him an habitation; my father's God, and I will exalt him. |

The number of praise Scriptures is almost limitless. Praise is a vital means of launching into prayer. You will find the Scriptures helpful in learning how to praise the Lord.

I have assumed that sins have been confessed opening the way between you and God. That being done, we are ready to intercede. Again, the Scriptures are valuable as an aid in intercession. Paul's epistles afford a rich treasure in praying for others. You will find your specific intercession well worded somewhere in the Bible. Though no prayer is entirely made up of Scriptures you will find praying the Word helpful indeed. An intercession sheet may look like the one in the figure. Dating your requests and answers will bring delight for years to come.

Your personal prayer program will involve all kinds of praying and will take an increasing amount of time as your prayer life grows. Your prayer list will lengthen. Your excitement at the privilege of prayer will increase. Your effectiveness in prayer will grow.

Have a specific time for prayer and determine that nothing shall keep you from it.

As you become an intercessor, you can become a part of the most exciting program in your church . . . its prayer program.

Two: there is the church program of prayer. I am not going to outline a full program of prayer for the church but I will make some suggestions for one that will transform any church. Several years ago when I began to have some real convictions about the primacy of prayer in the church I challenged the church for one week to experiment with around-the-clock prayer. We enlisted 168 people to pray around the clock, one each hour for the entire week. We had them come to the church to do their praying. At the end of the week we recounted the value of the experiment. The results were so astounding that we determined that we would never be without this prayer program as long as there was a church. The program is simple. I have outlined it briefly in the book *Much More.* I will simply list the steps to such a program here.

1. Get your church prayer-minded.
2. Challenge the congregation with the primacy of prayer.
3. Present the general outline of a twenty-four hour prayer program. This will involve fourteen prayer coordinators with one prayer chairman. The fourteen coordinators will be responsible for enlisting, training, and monitoring to fill one twelve-hour segment during the week. This will be done under the supervision and with the cooperation of the prayer chairman. Specific information may be obtained by writing the Castle Hills Baptist Church in San Antonio, Texas, or the MacArthur Boulevard Baptist Church in Irving, Texas. This church will provide you with an Intercessory Prayer Packet which will greatly help you in setting up a prayer ministry.
4. After the church adopts the program, find a suitable place which will be used for nothing else but prayer. You will not have any trouble in raising any reasonable amount of money needed for the prayer project. In Memphis, Tennessee, near the end of a revival meeting, I challenged the church to start such a prayer program. In one night they enlisted over 168 people and raised all the money necessary to prepare the chapel and begin the program. Within one month, the program was going full blast. This happened at the Leawood Baptist Church, Dr. Jerry Glisson, pastor.
5. Keep the prayer ministry before the people, giving reports of answers to prayers and allowing intercessors to testify of the value of prayer in their own spiritual lives. In the prayer ministry begun in Castle Hills Baptist Church, we have had many phenomenal answers to prayers.

One night a distraught man entered the prayer chapel where our intercessor prayed with him. His wife had left him and he had no reason to live. The next day he was gloriously saved. He enlisted others to begin to pray for his wife. She was soon saved and their marriage was saved.

During the Vietnam conflict, the husband of one of our members was reported missing in action. His wife called the pastor and immediately the intercessors began praying for his safety. Fourteen days later he was rescued and gave report of a number of miracles that happened during the days following a helicopter crash behind enemy lines.

I was praying in the chapel early one morning. It was one of those times when I was tired, and thoughts kept running through my mind as to whether it was worthwhile running the list of names, many of which I did not know, on the Rolodex file. The Lord knew I needed a lesson so about that time the door of the prayer chapel swung open and in walked a couple in our church with a guest by their side. It was a man whose name was familiar to me. He had been missing in action for five years in Vietnam, and we had prayed for him during that time. He said, "I just wanted to drop in and see the place where my name was called in prayer during my years of imprisonment!" I needed no more convincing!

Many have been the times when people called in over the prayer line and have received Christ as Savior over the phone.

The prayer ministry of the church is so much on my heart that whenever I go I seek to get a church excited about it. If excitement builds regarding the possibility of a prayer ministry of this kind in the church, we take positive steps to get it going. In the Travis Avenue Baptist Church in Fort Worth, James Coggin, pastor, I first presented the prayer program to the deacons. On the same evening I presented it to the Sunday School leadership. After one week of experimenting with the ministry, they declared that they would not be without it again. It is full swing today!

My vision calls for churches across the country with a concerted prayer ministry. Every church with an around-the-clock prayer ministry should have a list of all the other churches with the same kind of ministry. The special prayer numbers should be listed in every prayer chapel of all the prayer centers. The names of pastors, evangelists, and denominational leaders should be listed in the files. With a wave of prayer across our country, it would doubtlessly be a short while before Spirit-borne revival would begin to come!

After the Spirit comes, we will not need to pray less but more. Days of excitement and dynamic call for the stability of prayer. Teams of prayer specialists could be brought in to bear testimony and give know-how in establishing prayer programs.

May God bless you as you become involved in yours and the church's greatest ministry.

14
Spiritual
Footwashing

"Renewal Evangelism" is a new term for our day. I have not investigated all its facets but I feel very positively about the overtones of it. There is the positive implication that if we are going to have real evangelism we must couple it with renewal within the body of Christ. This is a chapter about the underlying philosophy behind real renewal.

JRT

"If I then, your Lord and Master, have washed your feet; ye also ought to wash one another's feet" (John 13:14).

Hey, I Have a Need!

After the Spirit comes in liberating capacity, there are excitement, energy, and effectiveness. It is a common misconception that this new usefulness brings such maturity that we who are thus used are immune from need. As long as we live on this side of his coming, we will have needs. We are in trouble when we get to a point that we do not think we have any!

A few months ago I got the spiritual "blahs." I tried to disregard the creeping feelings of discouragement, depression, and defeat. But try as I might, they were there hounding me day after day. I thought to myself: I know better than this! I know the secret of victory. I have written books on living triumphantly! I'm simply not supposed to have need!" And because I honestly felt this way, I wouldn't even tell my wife some of the things that were going on inside my head.

111

Could I have been mistaken about my salvation? This is how deep my misery was beginning to go. I had a problem. In fact, I had two problems. One, I had problems, and two, I wasn't supposed to have problems. (So I thought!) Now that's worse than just having one problem! Yes, I was saved, but perhaps there was sin in my life which kept the Holy Spirit from continuing to fill me. I sought to confess every sin up to date and ask the Lord to continue his filling processes. But there was still need! There was joy in prayer and liberty and effectiveness in preaching and service. Effectual doors were continuing to open, and I had the sense of the hand of God upon my life. But there was still need!

It was at this point that God began to do a new work in my life and in our church fellowship. I asked the Lord to guide my thoughts and studies. There was a strange preoccupation with the material in the thirteenth chapter of John in the narrative which tells of Jesus washing the feet of the disciples. I thought: Footwashing? Never! Not in my church! But I began to read and study the verses contained in the narrative and pray as to what message this lesson had for us today. We have no evidence that Jesus meant to establish footwashing as a church ordinance and I am certainly not advocating it here. What I am saying is this . . . *that there is a spirit and a ministry which underlies the act of footwashing which we must recover in the church today if we are to have renewal.* You may never have your feet washed by another. You may never wash another's feet. But unless we discover the spiritual vitality of the spiritual counterpart of physical footwashing we shall suffer great loss in the church of the Lord Jesus Christ.

I discovered this on the basis of my own need. I did not need to be saved. I already was saved. I had also been filled with the Spirit and knew no reason why I was not continuing to be filled with the Spirit. And yet there was need! What else is there past spiritual birth and fulness? Is it that fellowship of love between body members when spiritual footwashing takes place. It is the releasing of the love of God which is in our hearts by the Holy Spirit to others and receiving their love to our hearts. If you think you don't need this, you are sadly mistaken!

Before we get into the heart of the narrative, I want to remind you of a vital fact in the book of John. There are three mentions of water that are significant for our spiritual relationships. Frequent reference is made in John's Gospel to *water* as expressing life.

In John 4:14 Jesus gives a beautiful promise to a woman of the world. He says: "But whosoever drinketh of the water that I shall give him shall never thirst; but the water that I shall give him shall be in him a well of water springing up into everlasting life." This is the first function of the water of life . . . to satisfy our inner cravings. *This is the satisfaction of salvation.*

Then in John 7:38 there is reference made to an abundance of life in overflow. "He that believeth on me, as the scripture hath said, *out of his belly shall flow rivers of living water.*" The emphasis here seems to be on the *satisfaction of overflow and fruitfulness.*

There is a third use of water here in John 13. It is that of service one to another. *He girded himself with a towel and served them.* In serving them he, himself, was served. (Though he was the only one present who did not get his feet washed!)

Thus we have the threefold significance of water in the spiritual relationships. We have first, an *abiding salvation* depicted in the well of water "springing up"; then we have *abundant satisfaction* described in the *rivers* of water flowing from the inner man; and finally, we have the *abandoned service* pictured in Jesus washing the disciples' feet. This is the blessed balance of the triangle of victory . . .

Abiding salvation . . .

Abundant satisfaction . . .

and Abandoned service.

We have found the secret of personal salvation . . . that well of water that opens within when Jesus comes in. The woman came to the well for a drink and before the experience was over she went home with the well inside her! We have found the secret of personal satisfaction. Having thirsted, come, drunk, and believed, we have discovered the rivers flowing out from the inner man. But have we discovered the secret of refreshing and renewal suggested through the spiritual implications of Jesus' act of washing the feet of his disciples?

Let me repeat . . . IF THE SPIRIT, HAVING COME, IS TO CONTINUE TO HAVE HIS WAY, WE MUST LEARN THE SPIRITUAL COUNTERPART OF PHYSICAL FOOTWASHING!

Now let us look to the narrative in John 13. The chapter opens with the declaration that Jesus knew that his hour was come. The coming events of his death were crowding into his mind. He knew that the Father had given all things into his hands . . . that he had come from God and was about to go back to God. Though he was certain of all things, he still had needs and knew that his disciples had needs. He knew that he was about to leave them and that they were not equipped to understand his coming death. He would tell them as much as they could take a little while later as he introduced the Comforter, the blessed Holy Spirit. But they would not understand! His feeling for them was described in John 13:1, "Having loved his own which were in the world, he loved them unto the end." His was a "terminal love" for them!

Then the narrative records an event which left the disciples gasping in shock and surprise. They watched him as he arose from supper and laid aside his outer garment and girded himself with a towel. He filled a basin with water and began, without a word, to wash the disciples' feet and wipe them with the towel.

Right at this point I want to say three things that I believe to be significant about Jesus washing the disciples' feet.

First, love was the reason. Search if you will, but you will find only one motive for Jesus doing what he did . . . LOVE! His actions were not brought about by their sinfulness but by his overflowing love that would vitally minister to them.

Second, renewal was the result. In the first place, their feet were weary from travel and dusty from the paths they had trod. It was surely refreshing to the disciples physically to have their weary feet bathed. But in the very act of washing their feet, Jesus was interceding for them, pouring out his love to them individually, and leaving the refreshment of his nearness in their hearts. They were physically and spiritually renewed.

Third, service was the end. When Jesus was through washing their feet, he asked, "Do you know what I have done to you?" Then he said, "Ye call me Master and Lord: and ye say well; for so I am. If I then, your Lord and Master, have washed your feet; ye also ought to wash one another's feet. For I have given you an example, that ye should do as I have done to you." By saying this Jesus put the ministry in their hands. It was not to stop with that event. They were to perpetuate the ministry of renewal by washing one another's feet. Thus they would serve one another.

An Explanation

I am so desirous of your getting the point behind footwashing that I feel obligated to keep emphasizing this point. *The physical act is not nearly so important as the spirit underlying it.* In the culture of the day in which Jesus walked the earth, footwashing was fitting. It was not, however, normally done by superiors or equals in society but by servants. Culturally it does not seem to be ordinarily fitting in our society. (Though it might serve to teach us humility!)

Why the feet? The feet are the lowest extremity of the human body. Humility, bending the lowest, would stop at the feet . . . the humblest part of the human body. Not only this but they are a necessary part of the human body. They are necessary to mobility. They are the means of going. Have your feet ever hurt you and it felt like you were hurting all over? Have you then known the refreshing experience of dangling them in a quiet, cool, refreshing stream or soaking them in hot water or soothing them with ointment? Your traveling gear had been renewed!

So while Jesus in the flesh was taking a towel, filling the basin, and washing the disciples' feet . . . HE WAS IN THE SPIRIT GIRDING HIMSELF WITH A TOWEL OF HUMILITY, TAKING THE BASIN AND FILLING IT WITH LOVE, AND RENEWING THE SPIRITS OF THE DISCIPLES!

Can you imagine that moving scene. He who had calmed the mighty tempest, stood boldly against his enemies, spoke with such authority that demons fled, and spoke words that raised the dead . . . NOW WASHES THE DISCIPLES' FEET. Surely they are weeping now though they do not understand. Something is happening inside their hearts that they will be able to comprehend much better a little later. A strange new strength is rising inside them. As Jesus bends to wash their feet, his eyes rise to meet theirs. He knows that the time will come when he is no longer with them. They will grow weary and discouraged. Their feet will be tired and will drag. But then as he would go on . . . Peter poses a problem!

Peter's Protest

Peter's protest is both interesting and significant. It may well give us a clue to many of our own spiritual problems. When Jesus came to Peter to wash his feet, instead of giving silent consent as did the other disciples, Peter protested, "Lord, dost thou wash my feet?" Jesus said, "What I do now, you will not understand until later." Peter replied, "Lord thou shalt never wash my feet."

Let's examine that refusal for a moment. What did it mean? What does it tell us about Peter's spiritual condition? Was it an act of humility or an act of pride? Primarily, it was an act of ignorance. But don't blame Peter . . . he just put into words what many of the others were feeling. He may have had the advantage of more open honesty than they.

He may have been saying, "Lord, I don't have a need to have my feet washed! These others may need it but not I! I am spiritually mature and well in charge of the situation." That would have been pride.

He may have been saying, "Lord, I'm so wretched . . . I don't deserve to have my feet washed by you. I'm so much less than the rest of the disciples." This would have been humility.

Whatever his response meant . . . *the point is that Peter missed the point.* He missed it even worse when he tried to recover after Jesus made the shocking declaration, "If I wash thee not, thou hast no part with me!" Peter's reply in that case was, "Lord, not my feet only, but also my hands and my head!" Jesus sought to explain, "If you have already bathed, you don't need another bath . . . but your feet do need to be washed" (Personal translation).

Peter evidently capitulated and allowed Jesus to wash his feet. By doing so, he was receiving the love of Jesus and saying, "I need!" I wouldn't be at all surprised but that Peter got more out of that footwashing than anyone there that day!

And you know, the moment I became honest about my need with the Lord, I experienced a spiritual footwashing! I was renewed and it started when I simply said, "Lord, I have a need!" It was so comforting to feel that I was not being chided for having a need. It was as if Jesus was saying: "I understand . . . life is like that! Take off your shoes and socks and let me just love you. No sermons

. . . no lectures . . . no little catchy phrases . . . just love! Not a command to get a little busier, or read four chapters in the Bible, or pray a little longer . . . just love!" And I experienced spiritual footwashing! Life had lost its freshness and needed the renewing of love.

And on the heels of that experience, I found that just as I needed to have my spiritual footwashing I needed to minister to others in the same way he ministered to me. I found myself willing and with a great deal of feeling to take a literal towel and a literal basin and begin washing feet! As I would feature it in my mind I would begin to weep. I thought of folks who had spoken against me, folks who had been such a blessing to me, and my family. In my spirit I went on a footwashing crusade. My imagination would carry me to a friend and there I would wash that friend's feet. Maybe there was forgiveness to be asked, gratitude to be shared, or just love to be poured out. It was a season of unparallelled blessing!

One Sunday I preached on spiritual footwashing in our church. The results were enheartening and immediate. We did not have literal footwashing but there was spiritual footwashing all around. One lady came by my office the next morning to say that she had been so busy washing feet (spiritually) that she hadn't been able to get anything else done.

While we prayed and looked for a new blast of revival from above . . . the revival began to come from within each of us as we poured out our love to one another! THIS IS RENEWAL AND REVIVAL!

Dear reader, you may have been saved and Spirit-filled and are now walking in the Spirit but you will find that at intervals you need your feet washed. You need your goings renewed! More activity, more giving, another testimony, or more determined discipline cannot take the place of this blessed renewal that comes from having your feet washed and ministering in love to others. Have you ever just gotten weary . . . physically, mentally, and spiritually? Doubt, despair, and resentment became your companions. Reactions welled up within you. You were your own worst enemy and knew it. You had need but you did not know how to say it. You go to one brother . . . and he gives you advice. He scores your prayerlessness and chides you for your discouragement. Everything he says is true, and you go away with some facts but no life! You go to another brother and he prays for you . . . binds the devil from you and gives you a scriptural formula. Your heart hopes but there is no refreshing. You come yet to another brother and mention your quiet despair and he says, "You too? Friend, I know just how you feel. Let me just sit by you and share your hurt and wash your feet!" The mood changes . . . tears flow and what formulas and prayers could not do . . . LOVE DOES! Then you reciprocate and take to yourself your brother's despair and wash his feet . . . and THERE IS RENEWAL AND REFRESHMENT!

Ways to Wash Feet

There are many ways to engage in spiritual footwashing. I am glad that it is not confined to a mere washing of physical feet. That would be rather limiting. When it is looked upon as a spiritual matter there is far more versatility in opportunity. I may wash a missionary's feet on the other side of the world by praying for him and perhaps dropping him a line.

Recently, one of my dearest friends and I were temporarily estranged through a set of circumstances that could be blamed on neither of us. It had seemed to worsen as time went along. The enemy would place all sorts of suggestions in my heart. During that time when I began to see the significance of spiritual footwashing, I became willing to get a towel and basin and kneel down before that friend to wash his feet. After the experience of being willing, there was no more feeling of estrangement in my heart. I knew that the day would soon come when we would face each other in perfect love. Sure enough, within a matter of months we sat facing each other at a table. I said to him: "Friend, you know our friendship must mean an awful lot to God since the devil seems so devoted to destroying it. I want you to know that I love you and will do anything I need to do to make things right with you in the Lord." There was nothing by then and both of us knew it. We prayed through tears with hand in hand . . . and without a towel and water washed each other's feet! Hallelujah!

I don't want to be accused of going off on another tangent and thus I have sought to say over and over again that physical footwashing is not a necessity. In doing so I do not want to leave the impression that it is never appropriate. I was in a footwashing service a little while ago. I had been invited to a church to speak. I had spoken on the principle of receiving in personal relationships. After the service, we were invited to move from the church auditorium to another room in the church. There were basins filled with water and towels. We were divided into family groups inviting anyone who was not family to join us until all were included. Then in our little group we had footwashing! It was done in the highest sense of dignity and propriety! (And . . . enjoyment . . . . I might add!)

I have bathed the feet of my children as an act of love and have been blessed as I interceded for them, knowing that their physical feet were symbols of a deeper need . . . that of spiritual renewal. I have had my children wash my feet and have been greatly blessed by it. I could almost recommend physical footwashing as a meaningful and continuing family practice. These days of late have found me shaken to the core of my being. Every anchor has been pulled in. I have resigned the church that was my life for almost seventeen years. I face a ministry of fearful proportions. The other night after attending the church I formerly pastored for the first time since resigning I was a bit melancholy. My wife had already retired but the children were up. I quietly said to my children, "Tam and Tim, Daddy needs you to pray for him just now!" They understood and we knelt together. I listened to them pray for me and got off my knees, without praying aloud myself, with my spiritual feet washed! Praise the Lord!

IT IS HARD TO WASH ANYBODY'S FEET AND LOOK DOWN ON THEM! It is equally hard to wash somebody's feet and hold a grudge against them.

Where the Blessing Begins

Whose feet needed to be washed more than any other's there that day? Whose feet were more tired than those of Jesus? Whose path was as difficult as his? Whose way was as flanked with demon hoardes as his? Who was facing immediately the hardest steps a man ever took? If ever a man needed to be surrounded with under-standing friends who would wash his feet . . . IT WAS JESUS! Yet . . . HE BUSIED HIMSELF WASHING THEIRS! Here is the lesson . . . IF YOU WOULD BE BLESSED . . . BE A BLESSING! If you have your feet washed . . . start looking for feet to wash!

Jesus is the only one who walked out of that room that day without his feet washed! But remember with pleasure that his had already been washed by Mary. She took a pound of ointment and anointed his feet and wiped his feet with her hair (John 12:3).

The blessing begins with you! Do you remember the spiritual equation . . . "It is more blessed to give than to receive?" Couple that one with Luke 6:38 which says: "Give, and it shall be given unto you . . . good measure, pressed down, and shaken together, and running over, shall men give into your bosom. For with the same measure that ye mete withal it shall be measured to you again." Have you seen the sign, "THE BUCK STOPS HERE!" I have a better one . . . "THE BLESSING STARTS HERE. BEGIN THE BLESSING BY GIVING OF YOURSELF!"

Feet That Need to Be Washed

There are *cold feet*. Some of God's saints have grown fearful about going on. They are hesitant and self-conscious and filled with anxiety. Their feet need washing!

There are *hot feet*. Some folks just have an awful time being still and stable. They just flit here and there like a flea in a frying pan. Their worst need is just to be still. Their feet need to be washed too.

There are *dragging feet*. Some folks have a hard time getting with it. They are sluggish and never seem to catch up. A good footwashing will greatly help them.

There are *tired feet*. Some of the saints are just worn down. They are weary-footed warriors. They have been loyal and their steps have been faithful, but an army is no stronger than its feet. Footwashing can strengthen these soldiers!

There are *dirty feet*. Some folks' feet have been soiled by the path they have been forced to walk. They bear the traces of earth's influence . . . the roughness of the road. Life has temporarily lost its freshness. They need a foot bath as well as all the others.

There are *beautiful feet*. The word says, "How beautiful are the feet of them that preach the gospel of peace, and bring glad tidings of good things" (Rom. 10:15). Your preacher needs his feet washed. The evangelist could use it now and then. The Sunday School teacher who faithfully breaks open the Book to you needs it.

Would You Be Willing?

Let's create an imaginary situation as we close this chapter. Imagine that Jesus is walking in the room where you are right now. He looks at you with that look of unconditional love that speaks more than volumes. He has at his waist a towel and in his hands a basin filled with water. Would you be willing to let him wash your feet? Would you be willing for the God of heaven to bow at your feet and caress them and care for them ever so gently? I believe you would . . . with tears. Imagine Deity washing the feet of humanity! He finishes and pauses for a moment. Don't let him leave! Would you be willing now to wash his feet? Imagine the privilege of washing those feet that walked the uneven paths of life on this earth for me! Imagine those feet nailed to a cross . . . for me! Yes, you and I both would be delighted to wash them . . . and again with tears! And we would . . . praising him all the while!

All imagination aside now . . . JESUS IS HERE! He is here by his Spirit, living in every twice-born man and woman, boy and girl. Jesus is saying: "Inasmuch as ye have done it to the least of these, my brethren, ye have done it unto me!" Let's face it . . . if you wouldn't let them wash your feet, you wouldn't let him! If you wouldn't wash theirs, you wouldn't wash his. Settle that matter with that brother or sister. Get a towel and basin and get at it.

When We Understand . . .

The last chapter of this volume will deal with the subject of evangelism. When we understand the significance of footwashing spiritually we will be equipped to evangelize God's way. I have had to face the fact that one of the great deterrents to evangelism is the quality of Christians in the church today. *When someone does get saved in the average church, we have to give them a few weeks to backslide enough to have fellowship with many of the other church members.* That would be a lot more amusing if it were not so sadly true! But once we find in our churches a prevailing spirit of overflowing love our evangelism will not just make saints . . . *it will make evangelists.*

Spiritual footwashing will do two things to God's people. *It will keep us fresh. It will keep us free!* We need both in order to evangelize.

15
Let's
Prioritize
and
Evangelize!

A number of things may be true, but if they are out of order or priority the effectiveness of the truth is greatly hindered. "That ye approve things that are excellent . . ." was a plea from Paul to put first things first. A person or church may believe all the truth but if the truth is out of sequence there cannot be optimum service. This chapter is a plea to prioritize! If we prioritize . . . we will evangelize.

JRT

"And this I pray, that your love may abound yet more and more and extend to its fullest development in knowledge and all keen insight . . . So that you surely may learn to sense what is vital, approve and prize what is excellent and of real value . . . recognizing the highest and the best . . ." (Phil. 1:9-10, Amplified Version)

A New Word

Someone said that there was no such word! I have looked in a dictionary or two and haven't found it. Well, there may have not been a while ago but there is now. The word is "prioritize!" I believe that it is a word that needs to be shouted loudly and clearly on the religious scene today.

I have discovered that it is not enough to allow the Holy Spirit to reveal truth and let it go at that. We must also depend on him to order our priorities. We can believe the truth every whit and be wrong in the order of emphasis we are making on it. It is true that truth is truth wherever it is. If something is true it cannot be any truer than something else that is true. But . . . it does matter a great deal how we put the priority of first truths in line. In other words, we may believe the truth, but if we major on the minors and minor on the majors untold damage will be done. Let me illustrate:

Here is an automobile. It has a carburetor, an alternator, a radiator, a motor, and an innumerable host of other parts. It may be sleek and new and have four hundred horse power under the hood. The radiator may be radiating, the alternator alternating, the carburetor carbureting, and the motor running, but if it doesn't have a steering wheel and thus direction the whole set of accessories might as well be filler for a flood control ditch. The whole thing is useless . . . in fact worse than useless . . . dangerous!

We have a situation in the religious world today that could drive a person to distraction. If we are going to come through it with any semblance of sanity, we are going to have to get our priorities straight! What is this thing called Christianity all about? Why are we here? Why are we praying for revival? What is most important anyway? Before I seek to begin to suggest some answers let me give you a rather fresh testimony from my own personal life.

I have just surfaced from a prolonged period in my life when everything has been put on trial. There has been a shaking of things that are shakeable. I am sure that there will be shakings until Jesus comes. During this time I have surveyed many areas of truth and many movements in our world today. I have heard men of spiritual depth make statements that sounded right and good. Then I have heard someone no less spiritual make a claim affirming the truth of the exact opposite.

I have heard scholars say, "No one can be filled with the Spirit without speaking in tongues!" I have heard others no less scholarly affirm that tongues ceased in an era past and all so called "tongues" were of the devil. I have been frankly frightened by the dogmatism of both. And this reference is just an example of a myriad of other things on which we are placing so much emphasis today. There are two ways of putting emphasis on a thing . . . one, by actively and enthusiastically promoting it, and two, by dramatically and determinedly fighting it!

To tell the truth I got pretty tired of the whole matter. I asked the Lord for an answer. God doesn't give me many answers without a struggle. And truthfully I am very glad for that. I get about as much benefit out of the struggle as I do from the answer itself! Praise the Lord!

What is the answer? LET'S PRIORITIZE! Let's put first things first! It will help to prioritize if we know what comes in first position. We can best know what comes in first position by recognizing what was first with our Lord. He makes that crystal clear in Luke 19:10. "FOR THE SON OF MAN IS COME TO SEEK AND TO SAVE THAT WHICH WAS LOST!" That, my friend, is precisely the entire reason for Jesus Christ coming to earth. That is the scheme behind the miracle of the *incarnation* and the miracle of the *resurrection* and all the miracles between, before, and since. Nothing Jesus did was an end in itself. *Everything he did was a means to the end of getting lost people saved.* The importance of what he did was always validated in the light of his central purpose of bringing sons to God.

He did not come to raise the dead though he did raise them.

He did not come to heal the sick though he did heal them.

He did not come to cast out demons though he did cast them out.

He did not come to elevate womanhood though he did.

He did not come to set up institutions though wherever he has been great and worthy institutions have sprung up.

All these things that he did were attendant to the main thing he came to do! I have been thrown back on that in my own life and ministry. Though I do not feel that my ministry in the main is in mass evangelism, I am an evangelist and so is everyone in whom Christ is acting as he desires.

This chapter may mean more to me than it does to you. But you may find benefit in overhearing what God has had to say to me.

I have been the route! I have stepped into many pits along the way. I have awakened to find myself on tangents that only the grace of God could deliver me from. I was saying all along, "But this is truth!" And it was. But the matter of priority was missing.

I have spoken much of victorious living and the joy that attends it. But I have awakened to the conclusion that the real evidence

124

of victorious living is not in an experience of joy, no matter how wonderful and continuous, but in what the living Christ does in and through us.

I have had much to say about going deeper with the Lord. In the process I have seen folks get so set in going deeper that they have "dropped out" from reason, reality, and usefulness. The whole reason for going deeper is to be equipped to allow him who dwells in us to manifest his life through us in such a manner that men and women, boys and girls will be drawn to the Savior.

I have even had some things to say about the devil and demons. I still believe that the devil is real and that we have authority over him in Jesus' name. I believe that there are demons in the world and that the church will have to reckon with the problem of demon possession more seriously before this age closes. But this is *attendant* to our main business. Some folks have read my book, *Victory Over the Devil*, have made a few truths in it all the truth they want to emphasize, and have lost their way. It is reported that one pastor who was intensely evangelistic lost his evangelistic zeal completely because of a new zeal for casting out demons. Is he guilty of heresy? Hardly! HE IS GUILTY OF IMPROPRIETY! He is a victim of wrong priorities!

There is a new emphasis on discipleship and healthily so. But what value is so-called discipleship if it does not result in doing the thing that Jesus came to do and sent us to do. There has never been so much talk on spiritual maturity and this is great if the end of Christian maturity is New Testament evangelism.

I have a passion to stand in the hearing of all in these days when we are divided over everything from infant baptism to closed communion . . . from tongues to predestination . . . from baptism in water to sovereignty and free will . . . and say STOP THE MERRY-GO-ROUND . . . LET'S PRIORITIZE! Let's stop talking in circles and start walking in a straight line of unswerving purpose.

Have We Agreed on What's First?

If Christ is living in me, whatever was first with him, will be first with me. "And when the life of Him whose passion for the lost led him to the death of the cross is lived in us, the same passion will become the normal attitude of our lives toward the lost, for we shall become a continuous 'living sacrifice' that they might live. This is at once both the test and the evidence that the crucified and risen life of the Victorious One is being lived in us to the point of personal victory. THERE CAN BE NO VICTORIOUS LIVING APART FROM A SPONTANEOUS AND ALL-CONSUMING PASSION FOR CONTINUOUS PERSONAL EVANGELISM." The statement you have just read was written more than fifty years ago from the prophetic pen of J. E. Conant in a little book with the unpretentious title of *Every-Member Evangelism*. Much of the remainder of this chapter is written under the influence of that flaming little book. I am convinced that it should be required reading for every twice-born person in the world today!

One said of this volume, "If every pastor and three church members in each church in the land were provided this book and mastered its contents, such a revival would probably result as North America has never seen."

What is so unusual about this book, *Every-Member Evangelism?* The principal point of greatness is that it puts evangelism and the indwelling Christ together and makes evangelism a personal matter.

We generally have three groups of people in the religious world today. The first, we will call the "inner life" group. They are long on the Christ-life truths and too many times short on real evangelism. The second group is the "outreach" group. They are long on getting people to Christ but generally short on the deep truths of the Spirit-led life. The third group is not terminally interested in either area and seems to be more interested in redeeming the social structures of the community. The thing that bothers me most about this picture is the inability in the main of the first two groups to get together.

One of the problems of evangelism today is that we are trying to do with a corporate structure what can only be done by individuals. We may train the witnesses and should, but the fervor of evangelism will rise no higher to stay than the fervor of individuals who have been convicted and committed to the central task of the church . . . reaching folks for the Savior.

A great new emphasis is being placed today on lay involvement in evangelism. This is needed! For too long the pastor has been looked upon as the one responsible for winning others to Christ. The tide now seems to be changing with more emphasis on the pastor equipping the laymen for evangelism. The WIN (Witness Involvement Now) schools have been helpful in spotlighting the laity as potential harvesters and training them with on-the-job approaches. With the added emphasis on renewal evangelism, great days appear to be just ahead. Conant said more than fifty years ago: "When men are struggling and going down in the waves of sin, the pastor is not the whole life-saving crew. There was a terrible wreck off the coast of Italy. The captain of the life-saving crew, instead of manning the life-boat, stood on shore and shouted instructions through a trumpet to the drowning sailors. The report that went to the government said, 'We rendered what assistance we could through the speaking trumpet, but the next morning there were twenty-three bodies washed ashore.'" And the church that uses its pastor as its speaking trumpet and fails to man the life boats with the entire crew and push out to save the lost who are going down, will be responsible for a great company who will one day be thrown upon the shores of a Christless eternity who might have been saved if the Lord's people had gone after them."

If the living, resurrected Lord Jesus is alive inside our hearts it is more than likely he will be doing the thing he died to do . . . bring sons to God. It is not *we* who win the lost by the *help* of Christ, it is Christ himself who does the soul-winning through the lives and lips of yielded disciples. When the Holy Spirit controls a person, he will be constrained, impelled, borne along, to go after the lost, command or no command. Personal evangelism is the priority in our day as it has been in every day since Jesus was here in the flesh. It has been, is, and will continue to be the plan of God for the church. We shall never find another to equal it.

But alas, how shall we motivate men and women to personal evangelism? This is one of our prime problems. In the main, evangelism is in most churches a fever followed by a chill instead of the normal heartbeat of the church. This is where an emphasis on the operation of the Holy Spirit in the individual's life coupled with a mature New Testament approach of outreach would win the day.

Again Conant said, "The disciples were therefore commanded to tarry until the Holy Spirit came to begin His mission of actualizing within them the indwelling Christ, and told them that then, and not before, they would become effective witnesses unto Him. They must be possessed by the divine power before they would be enabled to obey the divine command and follow the divine pattern. Human mechanics are of no avail here; it takes divine dynamics."

Christ's commands are always his enablings. What he commanded us to do, he lives in us to carry out. Evangelism is not something we do for him but something he does for himself through us.

We are long today on mechanics, and I praise the Lord that we have never had as much emphasis on evangelism or tools to encourage evangelism. But whatever advantage we have in mechanics and organization we must have *dynamic* or it all alike will be to no avail.

The answer . . . THE INDWELLING CHRIST! He indwells us by the Holy Spirit to empower our personality and be in us, to us, and through us all he requires us to be, do, and give.

So the Spirit has come into your life in a controlling capacity? Don't stop at the experience . . . go on to the expression. The Holy Spirit in control of your life will give motive and might to your response to the Great Commission. It is not the imperative of an external command that sends us after the lost, it is the impulse of an Indwelling Presence. We may be commanded forever to take the gospel to the lost and it will never move us, but when we are fully possessed and controlled by him whose life it was to save the lost we will go. Back of all successful work for the lost is an inward spiritual impulse; and back of the impulse is the Holy Spirit who produces Christ in us.

Again Conant said, "We shall consider the divine motive power behind obedience the Great Commission. It is Christ Himself, empowering us to live by His indwelling life, and impelling us to witness by His overflowing love. As we seek the significance of his indwelling life working in us, both the meaning of the cross and the method of taking it into our personal experience will unfold to us. Then as we study the secret of His saving love flowing through us, the impelling power of His risen life in our lives, and the compelling power of His redeeming love over the lost will break in upon our vision."

As we prioritize, we will evangelize. And the evangelism which results from the power of the Holy Spirit within us manifesting Christ to the world will at once not only bring men to Christ, it will teach them of Christ, and train them for Christ. It will not count its job done until the evangelized become evangelists.

In the wake of priority evangelism several vital and necessary things will happen.

There will be a rise in spiritual health in the evangelistic church. The active presence of Christ means the constant flow of his life through us to others. Paul said: "Whereunto I also labour, striving according to his working, which worketh in me mightily" (Col. 1:29). Spiritual health is the continuing flow of the life of Jesus through his body. While there is an outflow in the life of the witnessing Christian there is an inflow of Christ's enabling love.

Worldliness will be on the decline in the evangelistic church. Worldliness cannot thrive in the church where there is obedience to the Great Commission. A worldly church won't be evangelistic and an evangelistic church will not be worldly. The two do not go together. The best way to fight worldliness is with a positive program which emphasizes the two-fold life . . . Christ dying for us to save us from sin's penalty and Christ living in us to do the bidding of God in the work of redemption.

Evangelism will head off doctrinal problems. I have never seen an active soul-winner raising questions about the authenticity of the Bible or any of the fundamentals of the faith. Again I quote J. E. Conant, "When a man gets into personal, first-hand contact with lost men and seeks to win them to Christ, he soon learns how lost they are, and that the only great thing that will avail for such great sinners is a great salvation provided by a great Saviour. He will raise no questions about the doctrines of sin, depravity, hell, nor about the doctrines of grace, regeneration, and heaven. He will not listen when any one says that there are flaws in the sword of the Spirit, the Word of God, for he is using it and sees how it cuts. A winner who is unsound in doctrine is an impossibility, because the active inflow of the life of Christ makes it impossible."

Evangelism will bring material prosperity. The promise of the Scripture is that if we will seek the kingdom and God's righteousness all these things (material needs) will be supplied. Many have been the records of churches who have paid attention to the first priority and have found no problem in paying the bills and reaching across the world with their giving power. I quote Conant for the last time as he says: "Let any church that is having a hard time financially give itself, in the power of the Spirit, to every-member evangelism, and see if God will not keep His promise. They must go after the lost with no thought of money, of course, leaving that absolutely with God, but no church can possibly give itself to soul-winning without being blessed financially.

Evangelism will bring continuing and spontaneous joy. No one is happier than the soul-winner because his relationship with Jesus is rendered current every time he wins someone to faith in Christ. He is not easily discouraged and develops persistence. Just as there is a unique brand of joy in the nursery in the hospital with all the "new arrivals" around there is signal joy in the church which witnesses a constant stream of new births!

A final warning and challenge from out of the past. Sixty-four years ago A. H. Strong, the great theologian said, "When we cease to believe that men are lost, cease to privately urge them to come to Christ . . . the glory will depart from us! The church that ceases to be evangelistic will soon cease to be evangelical, and the church that ceases to be evangelical will soon cease to exist!"

In the first miracle Jesus ever performed, the record is that Mary told the guests, "Whatever he says, you do it!" The difference between the ordinary and the miraculous was that they did what he said! The difference between the ordinary church and the miraculous church today is simply a matter of heeding Christ's command.

Finally, brethren, LET'S PRIORITIZE . . . AND EVANGELIZE!